*Handbook of English Costume
in the Sixteenth Century*

THE MARRIAGE FEAST AT BERMONDSEY

by Joris Hoefnagel, 1568–9

A general view showing town and country folk. Gentlemen in tight doublets, trunk hose, cloaks or gowns. Ladies in Spanish farthingales and hats. Peasants in loose coats and the women wearing aprons and coifs.

HANDBOOK OF
ENGLISH COSTUME
IN THE
SIXTEENTH CENTURY

by

C. WILLETT CUNNINGTON
& PHILLIS CUNNINGTON

illustrations by
BARBARA PHILLIPSON

PLAYS, INC.
Boston

FIRST AMERICAN EDITION PUBLISHED BY
PLAYS, INC.
1970

Library of Congress Catalog Card Number: 78–113 741
International Standard Book Number: 0–8238–0081–4

Printed in Great Britain

Contents

Acknowledgments

Our grateful acknowledgments are due to: The Essex Record Office, Chelmsford; the Bristol Public Library; the Colchester Public Library; the Essex Archaeological Society's Library; the Exeter Cathedral Library; the Hereford Cathedral Library; the Society of Antiquaries; the British Museum; the Victoria and Albert Museum; the Rev. G. Montague Benton, F.S.A.; F. G. Emmison, F.S.A.; Donald King (Department of Textiles, Victoria and Albert Museum).

Preface to the Second Edition

For the second edition of the Handbook a number of additions have been made incorporating the results of recent research, especially in the field of working class and children's costume.

The entire Handbook has been revised. A number of new figures have been introduced so as to make the illustrations more fully representative. Care has been taken to check references and the bibliography has been brought up to date.

I am greatly indebted to Miss Catherine Lucas, M.Sc. for research, for writing the section on working people's dress, and for all the work she has carried out in revising the text and illustrations.

PHILLIS CUNNINGTON
York, 1969

Introduction

The great Tudor century, rising from the ashes of the Middle Ages, glowed with a splendid virility. A new world of wealth and learning was unfolding. A new aristocracy replaced ancient families exterminated in the Wars of the Roses. The spoils of the Church were gathered round the Throne, and the Court naturally attracted wasps and butterflies. As might be expected, fashions emanating from that centre were extravagantly novel, gaudy and vulgar.

To get into the charmed circle, one had to push hard and the new Gentleman aimed at appearing emphatically male with massive trunk, pugnaciously broad-shouldered, appropriate for elbowing a way to the front. Never were fashions more suited to a monarch than those which adorned the person and reign of Henry the Eighth. They gave all men wearing them an artificial burliness and so dominating was the masculinity of this mode that for perhaps the only time in our history, men's fashions over-powered and outshone women's.

In that world of turbulent males, woman's role was static; she cultivated a poise of immobility, rigidly enforced by garments of substance and weight. All through the century, indeed, it seems to have been a feature of feminine fashions to have every joint of the body gripped and fixed by the costume. This artificial restraint in clothing has always signified social superiority, and few periods have employed the device so conspicuously as the Tudor.

In the second half of the century it affected the costume of both sexes often in very similar forms. Both enjoyed the restriction of an immense ruff, a tapering waist compressed by art, stiff in-flexible sleeves, and a fantastic ballooning of the hips.

Though to us the Tudor fashions seem to savour of fancy

dress, their spirit was, in fact, far from fanciful. Rather were they portraits realistic of a full-blooded generation, with a background of brute force.

Their fashions were heavily emphatic, very different from the preceding Gothic modes with their whimsical fancies and delicately pointed effects.

A modern writer has said that 'the Elizabethan age was pre-eminently one of activity'. This in spite of:

> *Thy bodies bolstered out,*
> *With bumbast and with bagges,*
> *Thy roales, thy ruffs, thy cauls, thy coifes,*
> *Thy jerkins and thy jagges.*
> (George Gascoigne, 1589)

As adornment of their Costume played such an important part in the fashions of this century, and as the various methods employed were so complicated and characteristic, it will simplify matters if these are described first before we proceed to describe the garments themselves.

Note

1. In the text, where references to sources are given in brief, full titles etc., will be found in the list on pp. 228–234.

2. In quotations, the original spelling is retained for all articles of dress and their features.

3. Abbreviations: B.M. = British Museum.
E.R.O. = Essex Record Office.

Decoration

AIGLETS (also spelt aigulet, aigulette, agglette, and numerous other ways. Very fashionable from 1510–1640's), were metal tags of elaborate workmanship, sometimes of gold or silver. They were often sewn on in great profusion, either dangling from points or in pairs with no visible tie.

'A cote of crymosin velvet with agglettes of gold 20 or 30 payer.' 1541. From Dress of Sir Anthony St. Leger, Lord Deputy of Ireland.

'A goodly youth wearing an hood with aglets spread.' 1590. Spenser's *Faerie Queene*.

BLACK-WORK [1530's–1630], sometimes erroneously called Spanish work,[1] was embroidery in black silk generally on linen. It was often worked in an all-over pattern in continuous scrolling, during the late sixteenth and early seventeenth centuries.

COLOURS
Indoor illumination being poor encouraged the wearing of bright colours, especially the primary tints. A certain shade of blue was used for the dress of apprentices and servants, and gradually blue became the recognised colour for them. Consequently in the seventeenth century it was avoided by those of higher rank. Pale colours were in vogue by the 1590's.

CUT-WORK (popular 1570's). 'White woorkes, alias Cutwoorkes, made beyonde the seas'. Sumptuary Proclamation, 1579. Imported chiefly from Italy, but by the 1620's was made in England. It was achieved by cutting out portions of the material and crossing the spaces with geometrical needlework designs. Pearls were sometimes threaded into the pattern.

[1] See Nevinson's *Catalogue of English Domestic Embroidery*, p. 18.

13

DRAWN-WORK (popular from 1550's). Also originally Italian. A selected number of weft threads were drawn out. Those remaining were whipped over and then connected by buttonhole-stitches to form a simple geometrical design which might be elaborated by the addition of darning stitches. Coloured silks were often used. It was popular for neck wear, shirts, smocks and night rails.

EMBROIDERY was very widely used during the sixteenth and early seventeenth centuries. Designs in coloured silks, gold or silver thread, spangles or owes might be worked on any article, including shoes and headwear. Embroidered borders and all-over patterns were common. Towards the end of the century designs were sprinkled with realistic flowers, animals and insects, such as worms, flies, snakes and snails.

'Froggs and Flies for the Queen's Gloves . . . .' 1581. 'Household Book of Lord North.' *Archaeologia*, Vol. XIX. 'He will work you any flower to the life, as like it as if it grew in the very place, and being a delicate perfumer, he will give it you his perfect and natural savour . . . . He will make you flies and worms of all sorts, most lively, and is now working a whole bed embroidered with nothing but glow-worms whose lights, 'a has so perfectly done that you may go to bed in the chamber . . . without a candle.' *Sir Giles Goosecap*, anonymous play published 1606.

FUR LININGS AND BORDERS were common for gowns and cloaks.

FURS used (see Glossary, 218).

GUARDS (1515–1580's, and less fashionably until 1620's) were bands of decorative material used as borders, or sewn on parallel with or covering up seams. They were of velvet, sarcenet or other rich stuff, but always different from that of the garment adorned, and usually of a contrasting colour.

Guards might be plain or embroidered.

'One cloke of fine clothe with foure guardes of velvette.' 1579,

from Will of J. Ayliphe of London, esquire. P.C.C. 11 Arundell
E.R.O.

'A chamlet jacket guarded with velvet, 8s.' 1569. Inventories
Records of City of Exeter.

LACE, meaning braid (as in shoe lace) was much used as trimming. 'A doublet of crymsen sattin, guarded wth small gardes of vellut (velvet) embroidered with lace of golde.'

LACE, meaning open-work fabric, was probably not introduced into England until 1545-6.

OES or OWES [1570's–1640's] were small rings or eyelets sewn to material to form designs such as S's or wheat-ears, or sprinkled over the whole surface.

'Dooblet of lawne cutt-work flourished with squares of silver owes.' 1589. Nichols. *Progresses . . . of Q. Elizabeth*, III, 8.

PANES [1500–1650's] were long ribbon-like strips of material set close and parallel. They might be produced
 (i) by slashing the material for the whole length, leaving only the top and bottom joined, or
 (ii) by separate strips, joined above and below. (See trunk hose.) In some trunk hose the panes were arranged so as to overlap at the waist. Through the gaps the shirt or a bright lining was 'drawn out'. 'Hose paned with yellow drawn out with blue.' 1592. Chettle. *Kind Hart's Dream.*
Puffs or 'Pullings Out' were the decorative swellings produced by drawing out the material through the slashes or panes. An indirect slash made by an open seam might be drawn together at intervals by aiglets or gems with a series of puffs in between. This was a favourite device for sleeves.

PICKADILS (the height of fashion 1548–1570) were scalloped or tabbed borders, a decoration very common for doublet skirts which were said to be 'wrought in pickadils'. At the end of the sixteenth century the term was transferred from the decoration to the object thus decorated, in the shape of a stiffened ruff support.

Square tabs or scallops, applied separately, were also in common use, especially for doublet skirts.

PINKING or POUNCING (1500–end of seventeenth century, in old fashioned sense. Very fashionable after 1545). Denoted small holes or slits of $\frac{1}{16}$ to $\frac{3}{4}$ of an inch long, cut in the material or in the finished garment, and symmetrically arranged to form a pattern. These were not 'puffed'.

'O, he lookt somewhat like a spunge in that pinckt yellow doublet, me thought.' 1599. Ben Jonson, *Everyman Out of His Humour*.

'Itm for welting and pinkinge of a french Gowne of vellat wth nyne thousand pinkes.' 1573. B.M. MS. Egerton 2806.

Pinking, in the modern sense of cutting a border into small scallops or angles, was used in the second half of the seventeenth century.

POINTS were ties with metal tags or 'aiglets'. When used for decoration they were made of ribbon or silk thread.

SLASHING (or SCISSORING) [1480's–1650's] denoted slits of varying length cut in any part of the garment and symmetrically arranged. The gaps revealed the white shirt, or a coloured undergarment, or, after 1515, a bright lining of a contrasting colour.

Sleeves were first thus treated (1480's–mid seventeenth century).

Slashing to other parts began after 1500, but was limited to the doublet until about 1510. The back seam of the doublet might be left open for most of its length to show the underlying shirt. This was an indirect form of slash.

Slashing was at its height between 1520 and 1535, being especially applied to hose and sleeves.

TUFFING OUT, TUFTING. See *pullings out*, p. 15.

1500-1545

MEN

THE DOUBLET (term in use from 1450–1670). Worn over the shirt, or waistcoat if present, as a close-fitting garment internally quilted, so that the lines of stitching were not apparent. It was shaped to the waist, which was high from 1490–1540, after which it returned to the normal level. The doublet was made with or without a skirt.

The Neck was

(*a*) Without a collar until 1540.

(i) Square and low, but steadily rising and often becoming oval [1500–1536].

(ii) Fitting round the neck [1530–1540].

Foreigners, children and countryfolk continued longer with low necks.

The Shirt was nearly always visible above the doublet, and at first was gathered into a low-necked band. But by 1525 it was usually cut high, and finished with a band fitting round the neck. By 1530 this was a standing collar edged with a turn-down collar or a frill, the origin of the ruff. The standing collar increased in height as with the doublet. Embroidery in black-work or coloured silks to shirt necks and wrists was very common.

(*b*) *With a standing Collar* (1540–1590, occasionally seen by 1535). This was at first low, but rose to its maximum height in the 1560's. It was always finished either with the shirt collar frill, which now was deeper and goffered like a ruff, or by the turn-over top of the shirt collar, also larger in size.

Fastenings for Styles (*a*) *and* (*b*)

(i) Tied or buckled on one side, generally out of sight.

17

1.

Doublet with low square neck, low-necked shirt showing above. Worn under jacket open in front, with sleeves of type (*c*) (p. 25). (1517.)

This was common with the low square necks until about 1530.

(ii) Buttoned, hooked, laced or tied down the front to the waist. Sometimes the ties, in the form of points with aiglets, were spaced to allow the shirt to be pulled out in between, giving a slashed effect. The doublet might also be left open to the waist, to show the shirt embroidery.

(c) *A deep V or U shaped opening* [1490–1520] to the waist in front, with a low curve round the back of the neck. This style, however, was far commoner with jerkins, and rare with doublets. The borders were usually guarded, but not turned back or lapelled as with jerkins. The front gap was sometimes laced across, but usually only closed at the waist by hook or tie. The gap was filled in simply by the shirt, or else by

(i) The *Stomacher*, or

(ii) The *Partlet*, (see p. 209) or

(iii) The *Plackard*. This, like the others, was a separate accessory. It covered the front of the chest, and was generally very ornamental. It frequently matched the detachable sleeves, and in wardrobe accounts was often listed with them.

'A doublet of black satin, the foresleeves and placard of tynsell.' 1523. Dame Agnes Hungerford's Inventory: her husband's 'Raiment'.

THE DOUBLET SKIRT

(a) *Absent* [1500–1530's]

(b) *Present* (from 1500 on, but always present after the 1530's, though often very attenuated after 1545).

Styles

(i) Full and covering the hips.

(ii) Shortened to a narrow flared border, often tabbed or scalloped.

A Belt was optional, but usually not worn.

A small Sash tied in front was occasionally worn.

SLEEVES

(a) Close fitting.

(i) Plain throughout.

2.

Doublet with low standing collar, open to show high-necked shirt with black-work embroidery, repeated on wrist frills. Full skirt; slashed sleeves emerging from puffed-out shoulder-sleeves of the short gown. Upper stocks or breech slashed. Prominent cod-piece. Narrow belt with hangers for dagger and sword. Flat cap with feather and medallion. Shoes with rounded toes and closed to the ankle. (1540.)

(ii) With a puffed-out fulness at the shoulder, or at both shoulder and elbow.

(iii) Full and generally paned from shoulder to elbow, then tight to the wrist.

(b) Wide, but sloping to a close fit at the wrist. These sleeves were usually slashed, revealing

(i) The shirt sleeve, or

(ii) The waistcoat sleeve, or

(iii) A sewn-in bright constrasting lining (after 1515).

Detachable sleeves (in common use after 1540). These were attached at the armhole by points, the join being hidden by an overgarment or a hanging sleeve.

Wings, or stiffened welts hiding the join, or covering the shoulder seam in the case of attached sleeves, began to be worn in 1542, but were only common after 1545, and belong to the next period.

Detachable sleeves might be of any of the styles mentioned. They were always listed as separate items in contemporary inventories.

Two Sleeves (1500–1580's) were occasionally worn at the same time, the doublet sleeve proper being allowed to hang loose as a hanging sleeve, while that actually worn, and usually detachable was of a different colour and material from the rest. It was called a '*fore sleeve*' or '*half sleeve*', because, as a rule, only the forearm portion was visible.

'A doublet of yellow satin and the foresleeves of it of cloth of gold and the placard of the same.' 1523. Inventory of Dame Agnes Hungerford, *Raiment of my husband*.

All sleeves were close at the wrist, with bands sufficiently wide to slip on over the hand, or fastened by buttons along a short vertical slit.

Shirt Sleeve Frills [1530's] began to appear below the doublet sleeve, at the wrist, in the 1530's.

Doublet Materials (among the fashionable). Velvet, satin, cloth of gold, and equally rich linings.

'A doublet of purple satten embroidered with pirles of damaske gold and silver.' 1547. Henry VIII's Wardrobe Inventory.

3.

Doublet with standing collar (the shirt neck frill showing above) buttoned down the front. Deep skirt. Sleeves with slashed design, and shirt sleeves with frill emerging at the wrist. Gown medium length with fur border and hanging sleeves. Upper stocks matching doublet sleeves. Flat cap and feather. (*c.* 1546.)

Doublets were usually of a contrasting colour which harmonised with the hose. A 'suit of apparel' might, as a minimum, consist of doublet and hose, both being indispensable.

Attachment of Hose, or Trussing the Points

Along the lower border of the body of the doublet (or waist-coat) were pairs of eyelet holes, corresponding with similar pairs along the waist line of the hose. Points (ties) were threaded through these opposite pairs of holes and knotted in a series of half bows or bows, encircling the waist. These were either visible, being tied on the outside; or concealed, being tied on the under surface of the doublet.

Visible *or* Concealed [1490–1560].

Concealed [1560–1610].   Visible [1610–1630].

Their points being broken
Down fell their hose.   1. *Henry IV*, II, iv, l. 242.

Points or ties were tipped with *aiglets*, which were ornamental metal tags. Points were listed as 'tagged' or 'untagged', but were always tagged when worn by the fashionable world.

Points were made of linen or silk thread, or ribbon. The price varied from 3d. to 3s. a dozen, not including aiglets.

Strong cord or *leather points* of the fifteenth century persisted among the poorer classes.

THE JACKET OR JERKIN,[1] worn over the doublet, had a fairly close fitting body, with high waist (like the doublet) until 1540, and a full skirt, varying in length, but always covering that of the doublet. It was lined but not padded.

The Body (including the neck and fastenings)

(a) [1490–1540].

Made with a deep V or U opening to the waist in front, the gap being bridged by the doublet or a plackard, and after 1500 rarely laced across. The V was edged with revers, broadening upwards and continued over the shoulders to form a flat falling collar behind, which might be   (i) Round (to 1510).   (ii) Square (to 1540).

---

[1] 'Jerkins', especially buff jerkins, were worn in the country, but Henry VIII's wardrobe contained no 'jerkins' only 'jacquettes' up to 1536. Thereafter jerkins took their place.

4.

Jacket with wide U-opening to waist, revealing doublet decorated with slashing and puffs. Skirt full and deep, hiding upper stocks. Sash girdle and hanger for dagger. No sleeves. The decorated doublet sleeves emerge from the gown sleeves, which are puffed out and have hanging sleeves behind. Gown bordered and lined with fur. Bonnet with halo brim bordered with ostrich tips. Shoes with square toes and slashed design. (1539.) (A *shamew* was probably a gown of the above type.)

(iii) With a step separating the square collar from the revers [1510–1540].

The U was usually guarded only. Either U or V was closed at waist only, probably by hook and eye and sometimes worn with a narrow girdle.

(*b*) Double-breasted, with a low cut wrap-over front and wide lapels. It was tied or buckled at one side [1500–1545]. Rare in England.

(*c*) The body was closed down the front by lacing, buttons, hooks and eyes, or ties. It might be left open. The neck was square or round without a collar. A low stand-up collar was added in the 1540's, and increased in height like that of the doublet.

The Skirt was very full, and open in front.

Skirts might be made up of strips of different alternating material, producing a striped effect. This was popular during the early years of the period.

Length varied from reaching to the knee or just below, to covering the hips. The shorter mode was more usual after 1530.

Bases [1490–1540] were skirts worn on horseback, with or without armour and were separate articles. Henry VIII had bases and horse's trappers in matching sets.

Length

      (i) to knee joint or just below (to 1518).

      (ii) Above knee (to 1540).

Sleeves

    (*a*) Absent [1490–1620, when the jerkin came to an end].

    (*b*) Long and tubular [1490–1515].

    (*c*) Full to the elbow, then close fitting to the wrist and buttoned [1510–1545].

    (*d*) Full to the elbow with no extension.

      Both (*c*) and (*d*) often had attached hanging sleeves [1510–1545].

    (*e*) Hanging Sleeves, were wide and tubular, with a large opening in front for the arm (1490–1600 and on). These apertures were

      (i) Long vertical slits.

(ii) Horizontal slits.

(iii) T or + shaped slits.

They might be placed at shoulder, elbow or wrist level, the first being by far the commonest. Hanging sleeves were sometimes worn in the ordinary way and ceased to hang.

Decoration of Jackets was less elaborate than that for the doublet, though all varieties were used. Slashing began about 1510. Leather 'jerkins' could be worn by country gentlemen.

The Chammer, Chymer or *Shamew* (1518–1540's) was a richly decorated gown or coat worn open in front, furred and lined. The sword was just coming into fashion as an adjunct to civilian dress and as it was still hung almost vertically from the girdle over the doublet the hilt was very liable to chafe the lining of the skirts of the shamew.

'Your swords freateth the plyghtes of your chymer.' (1530. Palsgrave.)

THE PETTICOTE (later 'waistcoat') was a waist-length under-doublet, usually quilted, and worn with or without sleeves, which might be detachable. It was never worn without the doublet except as négligé.

'Next your sherte use you to were a petycote of skarlet . . . made of stammel or linsye-wolsye'. 1542. Boorde *Dyetary of Helth*. 'Two petticootes of white taffata lined with the same.' 1535–6. Henry VIII, Wardrobe Account.

Hose were fastened to the waistcoat, when worn, in the method already described for the doublet as 'trussing the points'.

THE GOWN, worn over the doublet or jerkin, was broad-shouldered and loose, made with ample folds falling from a fitting yoke. It was open down the front, the edges having a turned-back border which broadened over the shoulders to form, behind, a flat square or rounded collar known as a *Cape*.

'A gown with a square cape, of crimson vellet and crimson

5.

Long gown faced with fur; hanging sleeves with horizontal slit and doublet sleeves emerging. Neck and wrists finished with shirt frills. Sash belt to doublet. Short hair with long full beard and moustache. Shoes with rounded toes, slashed uppers, closed towards the ankle. (1538.)

satten all over embrawdered . . . one gowne with a cape furred with Sables.' 1547. Wardrobe Inventory of Henry VIII.

Alternatively the revers merged into a rolled collar, without expanding into a cape (the gown of the serjeant-at-law had a hood). The Gown was worn either hanging free, or bound at the waist by girdle or sash tied in front, and sometimes also fastened by points from neck to waist.

Length

A *Demigown* was short, to the knee or just above. It was very popular from 1500–1560's, and often worn on horseback.

'My short rydinge gown of worsett.' 1548. Wills and Inventories of Northern Counties.

A Long Gown

To mid-calf for warmth.

To ankle for ceremonial purposes, general use or as a dressing gown. 'my long night gowne.' 1542. North Country Wills. Also on festive occasions: the future Henry VIII, aged 10, 'perceiving himself to be accombred with his clothes, suddenly cast off his gowne, and danced in his jackett.' 1501. Leland's *Collectanea*, v., 361.

Sleeves

(i) Full, with wide expansion towards the wrist, where sometimes turned back into a broad cuff with a decorated lining [1500–1520].

(ii) Long, full and tubular, usually worn as a hanging sleeve, having a vertical or horizontal slit in front for the passage of the arm. Worn normally when used as a dressing gown.

(iii) A puffed-out shoulder sleeve, with or without an attached hanging sleeve, or continued straight to wrist and worn normally [1530–1600 and on].

Mourning

Black gowns and black hoods were worn by men at funerals. 'To make them gownes and hodes after the maner and facon (fashion) of morners accustomed about such lyke buryalle . . . I wille that everyone of my children have gownes and hodes of blake clothe . . . and every other gentleman and yeoman.' 1529. Will of Sir David Owen (*Sussex Arch. Coll.*, Vol. VII).

a

b

6.

(a) Long gown faced and lined with fur. Sleeves full and wide at the wrist. Hair long to shoulders; clean-shaven face. (*c.* 1510.) (b) Medium-long gown with hanging sleeves and long vertical slits through which emerge the doublet sleeves wide to the elbow and tight to the wrist. Doublet neck rounded and low with shirt showing above. Hair medium long. Shoes square-toed; ankle straps. (1532.)

Materials. Velvet, damaske, chamlett, cloth, frieze, tawny, worsted, satin, russet or marble.

Gowns were usually (though not always) lined and faced with rich materials or fur.

Furs used. Black lamb, black shanks, fox, calaber, budge, fitch, cony, grays, mink. 'A new black gown faced with budge and lined with lambe, £5 10 0.' 1591. Inventory from Records of City of Exeter. (See also FURS, pp. 218–220).

THE CLOAK was worn over the jerkin or doublet for warmth or travelling. It was, however, uncommon, the gown being preferred in the first half of the century.

Cloaks unfashionable [1500–1545].

Cloaks the height of fashion [1545–1600], ousting the gown, which became largely a professional garment.

Styles

(*a*) A full, square-cut mantle, with a deep falling collar, square or double pointed. Reaching to just below the knees. Rare [1500–1515].

(*b*) A short circular or semi-circular cloak, generally tied by cords over one shoulder [1500–1545], after which more elaborate.

(*c*) *The Spanish Cloak with hood* [1535–1620], but rare, and confined to Court circles until 1545. For description see next section.

'It'm for making of a Spanyshe Clooke of crymsen clothe of golde, embrowdered and lyned with crymsen velvette . . .' 1536. Wardrobe accounts of Henry VIII. 'A Spanish cape . . . tied with eight Troches of pearle,' Inventory of his Wardrobe, 1547.

THE TIPPET was a short shoulder cape worn with a gown, or later with a cloak; also the extended tip of a mourning hood.

THE FROCK, a word that has been used at different times for a variety of garments, and now frequently mentioned in wills. It was possibly an overgarment, like a coat. Those of Henry VIII comprised a velvet-lined bodice with a satin-lined 'base' and sleeves (Inventory, 1547).

'A jacket called my frocke.' 1527. Lancashire and Cheshire Wills, vol. XXXIII.

'A coat of velvet somewhat made like a frock.' Temp. Henry VIII. Hall's *Chronicle*.

THE COAT was always an upper garment, and probably in the nature of a loose-fitting jacket, adapted for the various occasions on which it was worn. In the following it was synonymous with the jerkin: Henry VIII in 1509 'wared in his upperst apparrell, a (coronation) robe of crimson velvet, furred with armyns; his *jacket* or *cote* of raised gold; the placard embrowderded with diamonds, rubies, emeraldes, great pearls and other rich stones.' Hall's *Chronicle*. Again, 'I bequeath my best cote or jackett.' Will of John Nettleton, 1554. Leeds Wills.

Like the Jerkin it was sometimes *sleeveless*. 'A slevelesse coote of blake fryesse.' 1519. E.R.O. D/DL F153. That the coat was not always close fitting and identical with the jerkin though a substitute for it, is indicated by the following: 'To Thomas Stoyle as much clothe as shall make him a syde (long or large) cote, a pair of hosse (hose) and a dublet.' 1522. Lincoln Wills. The *size* is also shown by the mention of 'my . . . gowne or cote', 1555 (Leeds Wills), and 'a klockyd coat of velvett and damaske', 1520 (Lestrange accounts), which would correspond with a gown.

Riding Coats might be hooded. 'I bequeath to Gylbert Pemberton my Ryding Cote off whyte Russett wyth the hode to the same.' 1519. E.R.O. D/DL F.153.

Coats were worn by all classes, and made of as varied materials as the jerkin (occasionally parti-coloured).

'A coat of crimson velvet laid under with cloth of silver.' 1523. Dame Agnes Hungerford's Inventory.

'4 yds of tryse (frieze?) for a coat for the kitchen boy, iis.' 1522. Lestrange Accounts, Hunstanton.

In Warrants issued by Henry VIII for articles of dress in 1517–1521 (MSS Harl: 2284, 4217), there are entries of coats, demi-coats, riding coats, coats with bases, stalking coats, tennis coats, and coats of leather, some with strait or tight sleeves, some with loose sleeves, and some without any; some 'furred for wynter,' some 'lyned for somer'.

'3¾ yards of white satin for a stalking coat and a bonet.'

'Three yards and a quarter of black velvet for a tenes coat.' 1517.

Nine yards and a half of green sarcenet were needed to line a full coat; 11 yards black velvet to make a Riding Cote.

The variations were obviously great.

THE CASSOCK (1530 off and on to 1660's), was a loose over-garment, essentially beltless, with normally shaped sleeves. See also pp. 192–195.

THE GABARDINE (1510–1560's as a fashionable garment) 'was a long coat worn loose or girdled, with wide sleeves' (Linthicum).

After 1560's it ceased to be mentioned as a fashionable garment, but it was made of stouter material and used against the weather. From 1510–1560 the rich had brightly coloured gabardines of velvet, satin, etc. 'My skarlot gaberden' was bequeathed to 'make her a kyrtell.' 1519 E.R.O. D/DL F153. Those of the poorer classes were made of tawny, medley and other kinds of cloth. It was a very popular garment with them.

LEG WEAR

HOSE consisted of breeches and stockings treated as one garment and apparently sewn together. Although changing in design, especially after 1540, this single garment continued in use until 1600 and even after, although separate breeches and stockings began to be worn in the 1570's.

Styles

    (*a*) Close fitting like 'tights' [1500–1540]. The upper portion, known as the *breech*, was sometimes decorated—

        (i) With criss-cross bands of material, plain or embroidered [1490's–1515].

        (ii) With small slashes and puffs in symmetrical arrangements for the breech, which was often of a different colour

b

a

7.

(a) Hose plain and tight; fastened by points to skirtless doublet. Early type of cod-piece. Doublet, low neck, slashed in front and fastened on one side. Doublet sleeves with long back slit showing the shirt. Demi-gown with long hanging sleeves. Hair long. Small round 'pork-pie' cap in hand. Thick over-stockings and instep strap shoes. (*c.* 1500.) (b) Hose with slashed and decorated upper stocks. Bag-shaped cod-piece. Doublet with low square neck, slashed front and fastened on one side. Wide slashed and embroidered sleeves closed at wrist. Short curly hair and clean-shaven face. Small 'pork-pie' cap on shoulder. (1532.)

33

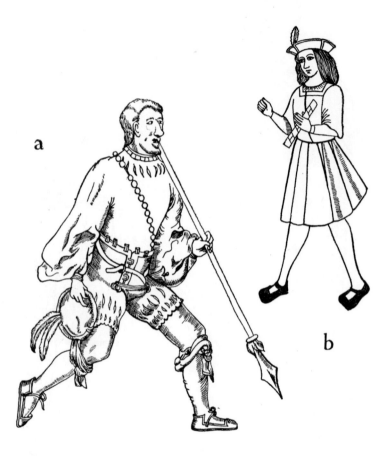

8.

(a) Hose with slashed upper stocks fastened to skirtless doublet; the
sleeves too full at wrist to be fashionable. Decorative garters. (1515.)
(b) Base-coat of a groom. Square neck and long skirt. Sleeves wide to
elbow, fitting to wrist. Broad instep-strap shoes. Bonnet with slashed
brim and feather. (1511.)

and material from the legs. These were usually plain, though parti-coloured, striped hose, or hose with asymmetrical designs, were common abroad and occasionally copied.

The Breech from 1515 tended to be slightly fuller, and varied in length from just covering the seat to reaching sometimes just below the knee, the demarcation being indicated by a different material. The breech usually matched whatever sleeves were showing.

Upperstocks indicated the breech [1515–1545].

Netherstocks indicated the lower or stocking portion [1515–1600].

'It'm for making a paire of hoose, upper stocked with carnacion-coloured satten, cutte and embrowdered with golde and also lyned with fyne white clothe, with two paire of nether stockis, the one paire skarlette, and the other paire blacke carsye.' 1536. Henry VIII's Wardrobe Account.

The term 'upperstocks' went out of use after 1550, but 'netherstocks' continued to the end of the century. For further notes on the form of hose and on contemporary terms see Appendix 1 (p. 205).

(*b*) *Early form of Trunk Hose* [1540–1560]. The upper stocks or breech, fitting above, were ovally distended from the fork to mid-thigh or lower. The distensions were usually paned. These were the forerunners of the true trunk hose (see next section), in which the fulness began at the waist.

The Cod-piece (worn all through the fifteenth century, continued from 1500–1575, and rarely to 1590, though there is evidence that in the country it survived till 1604). It was a bag-shaped flap at the fork, tied up with points, or, very occasionally, secured by buckles.

Change in shape [1515–1575]. It became very prominent and was often padded. It might also be slashed or embroidered to match the decoration of the upper stocks. 'He had on a plain russet coat, a pair of kersie breeches, without welt or guard, and stockings of the same piece sewed to his slops (upperstocks) which had a great codpiece on which he stuck his pins.' (A clothier, in modest costume, *c.* 1520. Deloney's *Jack of Newbury*, 1596.)

9.

Hose: decorated breech (early form of trunk hose) with prominent cod-
piece. Decorated doublet with very short skirt. Full cloak faced and
lined with fur. Bonnet with halo brim and feather. Shoes with slashed
uppers closed to ankle. Gloves in right hand. (*c.* 1540.)

Method of attaching the Hose was known as trussing the points, already described under doublet.

Construction. Most hose at this period were cut on the cross, with a seam down the back of each leg, and were lined. The material was stretchable in order to obtain a close smooth fit. Knitted hose were not made in England until *c.* 1530. (See footnote 1, p. 203.)

'Then must the long seams of our hose be set up by a plumb-line then we puff, then we blow, and finally sweat till we drop'. Harrison's *Description of England* 1577–87.

Materials were rich, and as varied as for doublets. Hose of the poorer people were of rougher textiles, and often footless, toeless, or stirrup-shaped.

GARTERS were small sashes or lengths of ribbon bound round the leg just below the knee, and tied in a bow on the outer side. They were worn for decorative effect. A length of two yards was common.

'Item pd for ii yerds of Rybband for Garters, ii*s* vi*d.*' 1522. Lestrange Accounts.

Cross-gartering began to be used, but was far more usual after 1545 (see next section).

SEPARATE OVER-STOCKINGS (1495–1505, then rare), later called BOOT-HOSE [1536–1680]. These were worn inside boots to protect the under-hose from becoming soiled or rubbed. They were large and loose, and turned down with a broad fold just below the knees. The earlier types were usually of coarse material. Boot-hose were not common until 1560. 'It'm for a paire of bootehoose of black clothe with two pair of sockis of the same clothe.' 1536. Wardrobe Account of Henry VIII.

SOCKS, probably worn with boots or buskins, and possibly used similarly to boot-hose or as linings (see p. 207).

'It'm for furring of a paire of buskynnes . . . for two pecis of reabande the one white and the other red, containing togeder in length one and fourtye yardes, and either peice in bredth three nayles ($6\frac{3}{4}$ inches) for oure sockis.' 1536. Wardrobe Account of Henry VIII.

Materials used. Cloth, linen, taffeta. Socks also of 'Geneva clothe . . . embroidered with silke and lyned with skarlette.'

FOOTWEAR

General Remarks

The shape of the toe was characteristic.

(*a*) *Duckbill toe* [1490–1510]. Square with rounded corners, becoming increasingly splayed.

(*b*) *Very broad, square and splayed* [1510–1540]. An order was issued in Henry VIII's reign, limiting the width of the toe to six inches. The change to round toes was not abrupt.

(*c*) Round [1540 on].

The most popular materials were velvet and leather, others being silk and cloth, all in a variety of colours.

Shoes of the slipper style had vamps made in alternative ways.

(i) In one piece with seam at the back of the heel.

(ii) In two pieces with side seams.

Soles were separate, and made of leather or cork. Soles of *felt* were used for tennis shoes. 'It'm for sooling of syxe paire of shooys with feltys to pleye in at tenneys.' 1536. Wardrobe Account of Henry VIII.

Heels were flat, raised heels being rare before 1600. The 'high-heeled' shoe mentioned in contemporary literature referred to high fitting heel leathers.

SHOES

(*a*) Fitting fairly closely, covering the foot to the ankle. (1490–1515, returning in 1540).

(*b*) Cut low over the foot, and becoming increasingly so, often leaving a mere toecap. These were secured by an instep strap and buckle or ribbon ties, or were worn without fastenings [1500–1540].

(*c*) *Closed to the ankle* again [1540–1575].

Decoration. Slashing very common [1510–1560]. Pinking more usual after 1560, both done in geometrical designs.

Jewels were occasionally sewn on.

Startups were high fitting country shoes, popular later and described in the next section. 'I give . . . . my schene (shoes) and starthuppes.' 1509. Lincoln Wills.

BOOTS AND BUSKINS were unfashionable, and mainly used on horseback or for travelling. (Also worn by soldiers.)

(*a*) Loose fitting and reaching to knee or sometimes higher. Generally slit for a short way at upper end of back seam to aid flexion. Tops turned over to display a brightly coloured lining.

(*b*) Well fitting (an Italian style). These were laced, buckled or tied by points down the outer side, more rarely in front or behind. Sometimes slashed at knees or ankles in a decorative design.

Materials, Boots were made of leather. Buskins, usually softer, were made of Spanish leather or velvet, and sometimes lined with fur—lamb or coney.

OVERSHOES

Galosh. 'A generic term for an outer shoe of several kinds, of which the patten was one.' Linthicum.

Contemporary descriptions all vary. 'A sole with latchets to tie it on.' 'A wooden shoe of one piece without fastening.' 'A shoe worn over other footwear.'

Pattens were worn with shoes to raise the wearer from the mud or wet, but they ceased to be a fashionable footwear as in the second half of the previous century. The patten had a wooden sole often made from the aspen tree, this wood being light in weight. To avoid unnecessary weight the under surface of the sole was sometimes carved so as to leave transverse bars under the heel and instep only.

Leather pattens with thick flat soles were also used. The patten was secured to the shoe by means of one or two straps over the ankle.

Pantofles (1529, but rare before 1570) were mules with toe uppers only, and were worn as overshoes (see next section).

Cockers were leather leggings, or high laced boots, worn by countrymen, huntsmen, and fishermen to protect the legs. 'His patched cockers skant reached to his knee.' *c.* 1514. Barclay's *The Citezan and Uplondyshman* (The Fifth Eclogue).

HEAD WEAR

General Remarks

Hats were worn indoors as well as out. Small hats, now generally called bonnets, tended to be low and soft during this period, i.e. 1500–1545.

1500. Small crowns with close vertically turned-up contact brims.

1505. Crowns expanding tam-o-shanter wise, and brims becoming saucer shaped and wider.

1510. Crowns similar and large, with brims extensively and varyingly tabbed and twisted about.

1520. Crowns flatter, brims narrower but still turned up.

1530's–1560's. The hat shrank in size and was perched on the head. Crown flat, brim small, untabbed, flat or drooping.

Types of Head wear

HATS

(*a*) A plain hat with a large crown and wide brim was worn by country folk and travellers unfashionably till *c*. 1515.

(*b*) *A large hat* [1490's–1505] with low crown, a spreading bowl-shaped, up-turned brim, and usually *trimmed* with a large plume of ostrich feathers, was worn at the back of the head, generally over an undercap. It was supplied with strings to tie under the chin or to suspend the hat on the back of the shoulders.

Trimming, with the above exception, was comparatively simple up to 1545.

BONNETS AND CAPS (alternative terms).

(*a*) *Small round Cap*, with close, vertically up-turned brim. (1490's–1520's, and with slight change, to 1600).

The crown was flat, round and shallow, or it was deeper with a soft curve over the top, often moulded into three or four lobes, and sometimes stalked.

The close brim (occasionally absent) was turned up vertically in contact with the crown, and might be complete, or slit into several portions, or divided at the sides only, or cut away in front (very common) the gap left plain or bridged by

10.
(a) Small round cap without front brim. (*c.* 1505.) (b) Small round cap with back brim turned down. (*c.* 1505.) (c) The same as (a), with crown moulded into lobes and brim fastened over the top. (1517.)

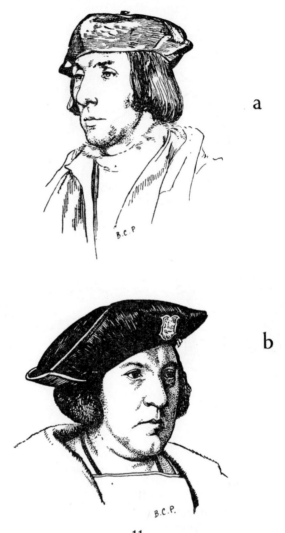

a

b

11.
(a) Buttoned cap. (*c.* 1530.) (b) Milan bonnet. (1527.)

ornamental lacing. A medallion or jewel was often worn as trimming—this might be sham.

> *High on his bonet stacke a fayre broche of tynne*
> *His pursys lynynge was simple poore and thynne.*
> c. 1514 A. Barclay—*Fifth Eclogue*, l.19.

After 1520 this cap continued as the *buttoned cap*.

The Buttoned cap (1520–1600 and after), was not stylish, but very popular, especially between 1520–50, for country wear, becoming indicative of a countryman. It was also worn by the professions and elderly men.

The crown was round, or sometimes square, and less shallow than formerly, and often beret-shaped.

The brim, absent in front, consisted of side flaps which could be turned down over the ears, or turned up and secured by a button or sometimes ties over the top.

Bonnets with pleated crown. All these were variations of a hat with a beret or tam-o-shanter crown, and a small adaptable brim. Intermediate types occurred apart from the main styles described.

(b) *The Milan Bonnet* [1505–1540's] was very popular by 1510. *The crown*, soft and ample, was pleated into a headband (tam-o-shanter wise). *The brim*, broad and turned well up, was slit on either side to form a front and a back portion which were sometimes united by aiglets. The back brim was generally supplied with tapes which were tied in a bow on the top of the crown. In the 1540's the brim was sometimes turned down, the ties then being absent. The Milan bonnet was trimmed in front or over one temple with a jewel, brooch or medallion. 'At that time [1542, a sort of] small gold medals were in fashion upon which . . . noblemen and gentlemen [caused] to be engraved certain devices of their own and they wore them . . . upon their caps.' *Autobiography of Cellini* (ed. Roscoe). 'My scarlet bonet w[t] a trew-love (quatrefoil)[1] of silver and gilt apone it'. 1508/9. York Wills.

[1] True-love is the country name for Herb Paris which has a whorl of four leaves with a flower or berry in the midst.

12.

Bonnet with slashed brim and medallion. Also shows low-necked doublet with embroidered shirt above, and gown with fur border and cape collar. (*c.* 1500.)

Usually worn with a slight tilt.

(c) *Bonnet with slashed brim* [1500–1530]. (Exaggerated forms very popular in Germany.) *Crown* of the soft tam-o-shanter style. *Brim* medium or large, cut into multiple sections or tabs, any of which might be looped up or buttoned to the crown. Individual variations were numerous, and the hat might be worn at any angle.

Trimming was elaborate, by laces or ribbon threaded in and out through slits in the brim, or caught at intervals round the edge; or pairs of aiglets might be grouped round the brim. Pheasants' feathers, or high plumes of ostrich feathers dyed in bright colours were common, and medallions were sometimes added. *Hat strings* passing over the crown and tied under the chin were also used.

(d) *Bonnet with 'halo' brim* [1520's–1550]. *The crown*, fitting the top of the head, was wide, low and flat, and again pleated into a 'waist'. The moderate turned-up *brim* hid the crown, encircling the head like a halo, and was usually bordered with ostrich tips, or trimmed with a single ostrich feather placed horizontally and drooping over one side. A medallion or brooch was generally placed over one temple, either on the up-turned brim or on the crown. 'A bonnet of black velvet and a brooch on it, cost 5 marks.' 1523. Dame Agnes Hungerford's Inventory.

This bonnet was worn with a decided sideways tilt, and sometimes over a caul (see Undercaps). Occasionally it was secured by a band passed round the back of the head.

(e) *The Flat Cap* (c. 1530's–1570's and unfashionably to 1630's) was a small round hat, 'cowched fast to the pate, like an oyster,' (A. Boorde), perched on the top of the head, and sometimes worn with a marked sideways tilt. *The crown* was flat and 'waisted' as with the previous bonnets. *The brim* was narrow and plain, though occasionally divided, with an overlap at the sides. It might be very slightly turned up, but was usually horizontal or drooping. *Trimming* often absent, though a small ostrich feather dangling from one side, with or without a medallion, was sometimes used, also aiglets.

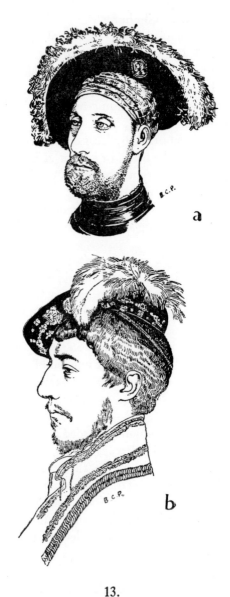

13.
(a) Bonnet with halo brim edged with ostrich tips and medallion trimming. Worn over a caul. (1532.) (b) Bonnet with halo brim embroidered, feather trimming and cord. (c. 1535.)

The flat cap 'by 1570 had become the exclusive wear of citizens and apprentices' (Linthicum), when it subsequently became known as the 'City Flat Cap'.

Hat and Bonnet Materials

Velvet, satin, silk, taffeta, sarcenet, damask.

Cloth. Beaver continued on from the fifteenth century for a few years, but was rare until 1580. Straw, Felt, Wool.

Knitted bonnets or bonnets of felted knitting were imported.

Thrummed hats rare (see next section).

Linings were always used, chiefly of soft silks or velvet.

UNDERCAPS

(a) *A Coif of linen* (a relic of the Middle Ages), close-fitting and tied under the chin, was now worn by lawyers and professional men only.

(b) *A Coif of black cloth, silk or velvet* was worn by elderly men under a bonnet, or indoors, and allowed in the presence of Royalty. Tied under the chin, or left unfastened.

(c) *A Caul*, or close-fitting round cap worn low on the back of the head, was made of a net work of ornamental threads, or of richly embroidered material.

NIGHTCAPS (ornamental), were close-fitting round caps, generally with close up-turned brims. They were worn domestically, but not in bed. They might be of velvet or rich material, or of cloth, and were often embroidered.

'A nightcappe of blacke velvett embroidered.' Wardrobe of Henry VIII.

'2 nyght cappes of vellvet for them (travellers) 8s.' 1547. Peter Martyr and Bernadinus Ochin's journey expenses.

NIGHTCAPS (plain) were worn in bed.

'Let your nyght cap be of skarlet . . . and in your beed (bed) lye not to (too) hote nor to colde, but in temperaunce.' 1542. Andrew Boorde *A Dyetary of Helth*.

These were sometimes tied under the chin with ribbon or laces.

14.
Flat cap. Hair-style of the period. (1535.)

HAIR

(a) *Long* to shoulders, with forehead fringe or occasionally centre parting. Face usually clean shaven [1465–1515].

(b) *Long* to nape of neck or a little shorter, with forehead fringe. Clean shaven face, though very occasionally a short beard and moustache was worn [1465–1530's].

(c) *Short*, but often bushy. Either clean shaven, or a short

48

b

a

15.
(a) Flat cap with stalk. Hair of young man. (1527.) (b) Coif. Hair of old
man. (1539.)

beard cut round or square, and trimmed moustache [1530's–1540's].

Exceptions, showing short hair, occurred earlier.

(*d*) *Short*, with long full beards and moustaches [1530's–1620], with changing styles in beards.

When beards worn, whiskers were generally present also.

An edict of Henry VIII, in 1535, is mentioned in Stow's *Annals* thus: 'The King commanded all about his Court to poll their heads, and to give them example, he caused his own head to be polled, and from thenceforth his beard to be notted and no more shaven.'

ACCESSORIES

GLOVES

(*a*) Had short cuffs, usually slashed or looped, and often of a different colour and material from the hand. The fingers were frequently slashed near the knuckles, so as to reveal rings when worn. These gloves were wide enough to be put on without fastenings, but were generally carried in the hand or tucked into the girdle. 'Hedging gloves' were plain.

(*b*) Gloves with long soft gauntlets were also worn.

Perfumed gloves from abroad were sometimes given as gifts in Court circles.

Mittens with one compartment for the fingers and one for the thumb were worn for warmth.

Materials

Leather, such as the skins of stag, sheep, doe, and the kid of wild goat called cheverel. This last was very popular because it could stretch. Also silk, satin and velvet.

The gauntlet was usually lined with silk or satin.

THE GIRDLE OR BELT

A narrow sash tied in front, or a narrow fitted belt fastened in front.

'It'm for foure pecis of coleyne reabande of div'se colours containing togeder in length fyve-score yardis, and everye pece in bredth three nayles ($2\frac{1}{4}$ inches . . . 1 nayle) for oure gurdiles.' 1536. Wardrobe Account of Henry VIII.

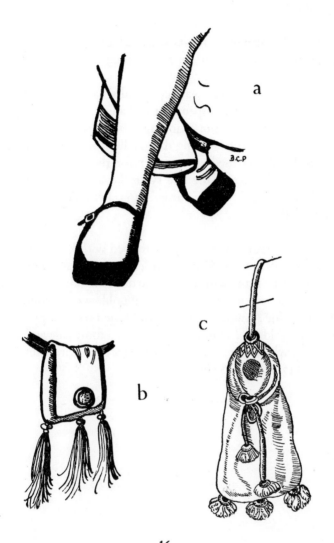

16.
(a) Toe-cap shoes with instep strap buckled. (1528–30.) (b) and (c) Two types of pouches.

Suspended from the belt:

A Pouch or Purse, made of leather or silk, usually embroidered. Drawn in by strings, often tasselled. *A Dagger* fastened to the back of the pouch, but in the 1450's slung from a tasselled cord which formed the hanger.

Short Sword, from 1500 was occasionally worn by civilians and more often later. It was suspended by a hanger.

Two narrow sashes, from 1540 might be worn thus: one round the waist, and the other falling diagonally from the right side of the waistband and used as a hanger for the dagger, or rapier. 'For 2 rapier bandes of the like sylke (Levant taffata) crymeson and white unedged, of one yarde.' 1569. Petre Archives E.R.O. D/DP. AGF.

WALKING STICKS, some very tall, topped with knobs becoming ornamental after 1515. Henry VIII left no less than 10 examples. One was a cane fitted with 12 useful articles including: 'a perfume of gold in the top, under that a boxe of golde wt. xl. counters . . . a Diall of golde . . . an inke potte . . . a Duste box . . . a penner wt. a penne of golde . . . a kniffe wt. a file . . . a foote rule and a compasse . . . a whetstone . . . and at the nether end a virall [ferrule] of golde'. 1547. B. M. MS Harl. 1419.

1500-1545

WOMEN

INTRODUCTORY REMARKS

Throughout the sixteenth century, a woman's dress typically consisted of her gown and kirtle.

'ii Damaske gowns garded wth velvet, and Kyrtles thair unto belongynge.' 1556. Lancashire and Cheshire Wills Ll. 15.

The Gown was always the upper robe, worn over the kirtle, and cut in one piece from neck to hem, or joined by a seam at the waist. It was usually rather voluminous.

The Kirtle was worn over the chemise and under the gown, or alone without the gown. At first it consisted of a bodice and skirt united by sewing, or very occasionally by points. The bodice was called 'a pair of boddies' (compare 'a pair of stays'), or the 'upper body'. The sleeves varied, but when worn under a gown, were always closed at the wrist.

A Full Kirtle was bodice and skirt (which need not match).

A Half Kirtle was the skirt only.

After 1545, when the bodice and skirt were made separately, the term kirtle came to denote the skirt only. This change in the meaning of the word did not happen abruptly, but for the sake of clearness, the above definitions will be adhered to, and in the next section, kirtle will refer to the skirt alone. In the seventeenth century the term became obsolete.

The term Gown similarly gradually ceased to indicate an over-dress, and with the dropping of the term kirtle, was often loosely used for a woman's dress as in modern times.

THE GOWN

Moulding the figure to the waist (worn high) it expanded over

a

b

17.

(a) Gown with low square neck; kirtle neck and chemise showing above. Sleeves with turned-back cuffs exposing kirtle sleeves. Sash girdle with tasselled ends; beads and purse suspended. English hood, early style. (1511.) (b) Gown with wide sleeves. Belt with triple clasps, beads and pouch. English hood, early style. (Style of 1500.)

the hips in the massive folds of an ample skirt, trailing on the ground and extending into a long train behind.

An alternative bodice was loose fitting, but usually caught in round the waist by belt or girdle.

Neck lines. Square-cut décolletage was usual throughout the sixteenth century, and the rule from the 1530's.

The neck was low and square in front, with a short or waist length V behind. The long V was laced across over the underlying kirtle bodice. The décolletage was usually partly covered by the higher kirtle bodice, or, should this be low, by the chemise, or by folds of material crossing the shoulders to form a V neck above the square.

Fastenings

(*a*) By back lacing.

(*b*) Down the front to the waist or just below, invisibly, and probably by hooks and eyes or possibly pins.

(*c*) The looser bodice was sometimes cut away in front, ending in a wide V below the waist, exposing the underlying garment over which it might be loosely laced. The gap might also be extended from neck to hem, when it was crossed at intervals by a series of ribbon ties. (See also placards, p. 210.)

Sleeves

(*a*) Fitting above, though occasionally loose, they expanded to a wide opening at the wrist where they were usually turned back, the coloured or furred lining producing a decorative cuff.

The kirtle sleeve emerged, and ended with a close fit at the wrist.

(*b*) Close-fitting to the wrist, ending in a turned-back funnel-shaped cuff open at the back. The cuff was sometimes turned down, extending mitten-like to the knuckles (a Mediaeval survival).

(*c*) Small 'bishop' (rare).

The Skirt, full and trained, was frequently caught up in two ways (up to 1525 or 30). Both might be combined.

(*a*) The train was turned up to the waist and there caught under the girdle, or pinned by brooch, or more rarely tied by

18.

(a) Gown hitched up in front with clasps from extra belt. Sash girdle
English hood, later style, showing hair in rolls. (1532.) (b) Gown with
trained skirt turned up showing fur lining. Square neck with buttoned
partlet 'fill-in'. Ornamental shoulder bands and sleeves with 'bugle'
cuffs. Belt with triple clasps, beads and pomander suspended. English
hood nearing the second style. (1525.)

points. Otherwise it might be slung over one arm. In all cases the lining, commonly of fur, was brought to view (up to 1525).

(b) The skirt might be hitched up in front by means of clasps (like nineteenth-century 'pages') suspended on either side from the girdle, or attached to a separate belt. (Up to 1530's.)

Trains for gowns and kirtles were fashionable during this period from 1500–1530, and less often till 1540.

'My violett taylett (trained) gown.' 1506. Will of Joan Holme, Derbyshire. Trains in front might be worn for mourning by ladies of rank.

Subsequently trains were only used on ceremonial occasions, or for weddings and funerals.

> *Ye wantoun ladyis and burgis wyvis*
> *That now for sydest taillis* (the longest trains) *stryvis:*
> *Flappand the filth among your feit*
> *Raising the dust into the streit;*
> *That day* (Judgement day) *for all your pomp and pryde,*
> *Your taillis* (trains) *sall nocht your hippes hyde.*
>
> c. 1554. Sir David Lindsay. *The Monarche* l. 5834–41

Linings for gowns was usual. Sir David Owen leaves to his nurse 'for good service, a gowne of satten lyned with velvet'. 1535. Linings of fur or silks and satin were used, and stiffening was sometimes added to produce the effect of fulness.

'11 yds of tawny satin for a gown for my mistress £4 11 8. 2½ yds tawny velvet for the same gown 33s. 4d. Roll of buckram for the same 2s. 8d. Stuffing cloth for the pleats, 11d. Making the gown, 5s. 1522.' Household Accounts of the Lestranges of Hunstanton.

'A gowne of bewti-colour lyned with black'. 1508. York Will.

Girdles or Belts were almost invariably worn. See Dress Accessories.

Decoration

Bands of velvet (guards) or other trimming usually bordered the neck, with a central band from neck to hem which might also be trimmed.

19.

Gown showing open front connected by ties, over kirtle bodice which
projects above with a square neck. A linen fold of material leaves a
V-shaped décolletage. English variety of the French hood. (1527–8.)

Short revers at the shoulders were common with the open gowns.

THE KIRTLE

Style (1). [1495–1530's.]

A simple frock, usually hidden by the gown, and having a full skirt. Fastened down the front to waist invisibly, probably by hooks and eyes. Occasionally buttoned or laced.

The Neck was medium low, cut square or round, or, rarely, V-shaped.

Sleeves

(a) Close fitting to wrist, with a small cuff, or plain and finished with the chemise sleeve frill. Slashing as a decoration might occur, either vertically, round the arm, or horizontally at the elbow alone or at the elbow and shoulder, the chemise sleeve being drawn out through the openings.

(b) Fitting at shoulder and wrist, but widening round elbow and forearm. Often vertically slashed. Finished with the frill of the chemise sleeve.

Girdles were usual.

'To Jenytt Eston, my servant . . . a kyrtyll . . . a velvytt gerdill with a sylver pendand and a bokill (buckle) of silver.' 1520. Lincoln Wills.

Style (2), with low neck. [1525–1560.]

Bodice was close-fitting and rigid, with at first a round waist, which began to dip in front after 1540.

The neck was square and décolleté to the shoulders, verging to an open V at the back. The front edge was slightly arched.

Fastened invisibly (by hooks or pins) down the left side from armpit to waist, or less often down the front.

The décolletage treatment

(a) Edged by lace, or embroidered border of a low-necked chemise. A massive necklace was usually worn which held a large pendant under the chin and after a double twist round the neck, disappeared into the bosom.

(b) Filled in by a high-necked chemise. This at first had no

20.

(a) Kirtle with furred cuffs and hem; linen folds at neck. Buckled belt with one long end tipped with metal tag and tassel. Purse and beads suspended. English hood early style. (*c.* 1500.) (b) Kirtle plain and belt with single clasp, and extension with jewelled end. Beads and purse suspended. Plain linen hood without the gable. (*c.* 1500.)

collar, but fitted round the neck and was buttoned at the throat with one button, the edge to edge closure below rarely meeting.

A low stand-up collar with a frill was added in the 1530's.

Black-work or coloured silk embroidery to chemise necks and fronts was common. (Also to wrist frills.)

(c) Filled in by a Partlet or a stomacher (see p. 210). The partlet was a separate accessory in the form of a covering to the upper part of the chest, like a chemisette. It was at first collarless, and usually buttoned down the front from a fitting neck. A stand-up collar was added in the 1530's.

'He cannot make a standing collar for a partlet without the measurement for her neck.' 1533. Letters and Papers, Henry VIII, vol. VI, 563.

The partlet was usually of rich material with much decoration.

'A partlet of white satin garnished with damask gold.'

'8 partlets of Cyprus cloth, 3 garnished with gold, the rest with Spanish work.' 1523. Inventory of Dame Agnes Hungerford.

Partlets and detachable sleeves often matched, and the set frequently made a useful gift. 'A partlet with sleeves' does not mean a sleeved partlet.

Sleeves

(a) *With oversleeve and undersleeve.* (Rare after 1560.)

The oversleeve, tight-fitting above, expanded abruptly into a wide bell at the elbow, with a deep turn-back cuff generally covered with rich material or fur. The cuff was often stitched up to the upper sleeve. This took the place of a gown sleeve.

The Undersleeve

N.B. Undersleeves were always closed at the wrist, and were frequently separate, being buttoned or tied by points at the armhole.

Types of Undersleeve

(i) Close fitting or moderately close fitting to the wrist. Might be plain or slashed, with the chemise sleeve pulled out into puffs and the frill emerging at the wrist.

(ii) Cut with a deep lower curve from elbow to wrist.

21.

Trained Kirtle showing front and back views. Low neck square in front, V-shaped behind. Oversleeves with immense turned-back fur cuffs. Undersleeves slashed along the back seam. English hood with 'tails' hanging loose. (1527.)

22.

Kirtle with low square neck and gored skirt open in front showing decorative underskirt. Double sleeves. Oversleeves with large turned-back cuffs attached near shoulders. Undersleeves with back seam open but joined at intervals by jewels. Chemise sleeve drawn through the gaps and chemise frill at wrists. A narrow jewelled chain girdle. English hood with sides and tails turned up. Rolls over the forehead. Brocaded forepart matches undersleeves. (1536.)

This seam was usually not sewn up, but caught together at intervals with ribbon, aiglets or jewels, the chemise sleeve being drawn out into puffs through the gaps, with the frill emerging at the wrist. The design was occasionally repeated for a short way along the upper seam. This was a stiff sleeve, sometimes quilted.

(b) *Without Oversleeve*

Very full, but shaped in to be closed at the wrist and finished with the chemise frill. The upper seam was often open for the whole length, being caught in at intervals by pairs of aiglets or jewels, the chemise being drawn out through the intervening gaps. This arrangement might be replaced by a band of embroidery. The lower seam was sometimes similarly treated.

The Skirt

(a) *Full gathered skirt* sweeping the ground, and trained until 1530 and occasionally till 1540. These skirts were sometimes hitched up in front by clasps suspended from a belt, as for the gown. Between 1530 and 1540 skirts became ground length all round, and the kirtle was called a 'Round Kirtle'.

(b) *A gored skirt* [1535 on] expanded in a funnel shape without folds from the small waist to the ground. A ∧-shaped opening in front exposing a decorative under-petticoat was usual, but rare with type (a).

A Girdle was always worn. See dress accessories.

Style (3) with high neck. [1535-1560.]

The Bodice was close fitting and rigid, with the waistline sloping to a slight V-shaped dip in front which developed into a deep point after 1545.

A yoke, generally of dark contrasting material, was common.

The Neck

(a) A low Medici collar, usually lined with light material, and leaving a V-shaped opening down to the edge of the yoke in front. Worn with a low or high necked chemise, the latter having a stand-up collar, generally embroidered, and always frilled. This collar might be closed in front, or left with a gap bridged by band strings.

23.

Kirtle bodice with dark yoke and Medici collar. Single sleeves, wide
embroidered and decorated with aiglets along the seam. Chemise frill
at wrist. French hood trimmed with upper and nether billiments. (1540.)

E

H.E.C.S.C.

(b) A low stand-up collar not meeting in front, but leaving a V-shaped opening below. Worn with and topped by the stand up frilled collar of the chemise.

Side fastenings, sleeves and girdle similar to those for Style (2).

The Skirt was similar to those of Style (2) though the stiff gored skirt was far the commoner.

DRESS ACCESSORIES

The Girdle. Three main types.

(a) A long narrow sash or cord, knotted in front, or occasionally passed through and held by ornamental rings, and ending in long hanging ends, usually tasselled. [1500–1530's.]

(b) A decorative belt, fastened in front by buckle or clasp often in a trefoil arrangement, and generally continued with one long hanging end tipped with an ornamental tag. [1500–1520's.]

(c) A narrow jewelled chain with one long pendant end in front, frequently sustaining a pomander. (See Accessories.) [1530's on.]

A Demiceint or Demysent, 'a half girdle or one whose forepart is of gold or silver and hinder of silk.' Cotgrave. That is, having ornamental work in front only.

'My dymescent of silver and gilt.' 1518. Will of a London Grocer's Wife (Wayman Wills).

The Partlet. Already described.

The Tippet. A short, fitting shoulder cape, dark with pale lining. This cape was often very abbreviated, and usually had a low Medici collar. [1525–1560.] Worn with Kirtle style (2).

The Neckerchief was a large white square, folded lengthways (not cornerwise), and used as a shawl for the shoulders, mainly with kirtles.

The Rail was a square kerchief of linen, net, cambric, lawn, or, with the poor, of coarser material, folded diagonally and also used as a shawl for neck and shoulders.

'Rayle for a woman's neck.

Crevechief en quattre doubles.' 1530. Palsgrave.

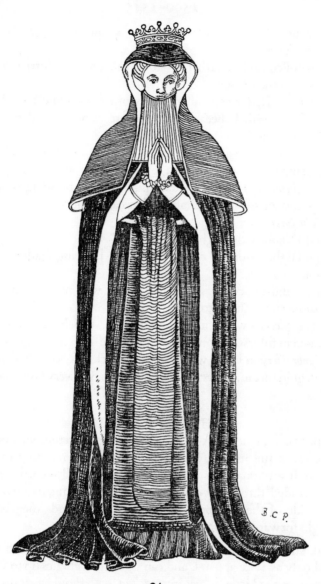

24.

Mourning garb of a Countess. Mantle black (with black lining) worn over black 'surcote' with its front train looped over girdle. Black caped mourning hood (lined white) worn over a white 'Paris hedde'. White barbe and hand-ruffs. Coronet. (*c.* 1576.)

'A course hempen raile about her shoulders.' 1592. Nashe. *Piers Penilesse.*

'A woollen rayle worth 12d' stolen in a country district. 1563. Assize File 35/2/3 Essex.

The Head Rail was similar, but worn shawl-wise round the back of the head. It became much more elaborate and popular in the next period.

The Night Rail was a cape which hung to the waist, and was worn at night or as a 'dressing cape' in the bedroom.

The Chemise, as already stated, might supply finishing touches to neck and wrists, and 'pullings out' in slashed sleeves.

   The Neck of the chemise

   (*a*) Décolleté throughout.

   (*b*) High, without collar [1500–1535], being gathered or plain.

   (*c*) Stand-up collar and frill, which was replaced by the separate ruff in the 1550's.

   The Sleeves were finished with frills, which gradually increased in fulness, becoming separate hand-ruffs in the 1550's.

   Embroidery in black work, red and black silk, coloured silks, or in gold thread, to neck, chest and wrists, was very fashionable.

OTHER GARMENTS

THE CLOAK, chiefly worn by noble ladies on ceremonial occasions, was a full mantle, left open in front, and reaching to the ground. It was usually fastened by a long silk tasselled cord, which was threaded through loops from jewelled ornaments sewn on either side of the low neck opening, the cord ends then being brought forward and loosely knotted in front.

THE SIDELESS SURCOAT was a mediaeval garment which survived only as State apparel, and can be seen on effigies up to 1520. Worn over the kirtle, it was low necked, with shoulder straps and large side openings, more or less oval in shape, reaching down to the hips. The front and back of the garment were consequently often very narrow. The skirt was full, and ground length or longer.

25.

Ceremonial mantle with heraldic designs. Corded belt to gown passing through triple clasps. English hood with hair rolls. (1524.) Another belt was described, in the same year, as 'a gyrdell of corne-work with a bokell and a pendant, the crosse damaske golde.' (Nichols *Manners and Expenses....*)

THE FROCK was also worn by women. Its nature is uncertain, but it was probably another name for a loose gown.

'my best ffrockke edged with tawny velvet, a tawney wursted kyrtle.' 1549. Durham Wills.

HEAD WEAR

Head-dresses were all low, and most of them were worn with undercaps.

(I) HOODS
   (a) *A plain draped Hood* [1500–1530].
This was draped over the head, falling in folds well below the neck, but having a ∧-shaped slit above the shoulders allowing the main part to form a curtain behind, with two lappets falling in front, these being the continuation of the face portion. At the angle of this division there often occurred a small decoration known as a 'clock' (compare stocking clocks).
   Round the face, the hood was either
      (i) turned back showing a brightly coloured lining, or
      (ii) curved well back, in both cases showing a decorative under-cap and sometimes a little hair.
Both (i) and (ii) were often edged with a broad band of embroidery.
   After 1515 the curtain and lappets were considerably shortened.
   (b) *A plain linen Hood* [1500–1545].
This developed into the 'Marie Stuart' hood, was similar to style (a), but stiffened to form an arch round the face with a slight dip above the forehead, it was curved in below the cheeks and there spread out over the shoulders. The falling curtain behind was often turned up over the head in various ways. The ∧-slit was not always present.
   After 1525 the side lappets were shortened and the 'curtain' divided into two formal bands.
   This hood was very common with old ladies and widows, who added a barbe or a wimple.
   The Barbe was a white bib of pleated linen, worn round the

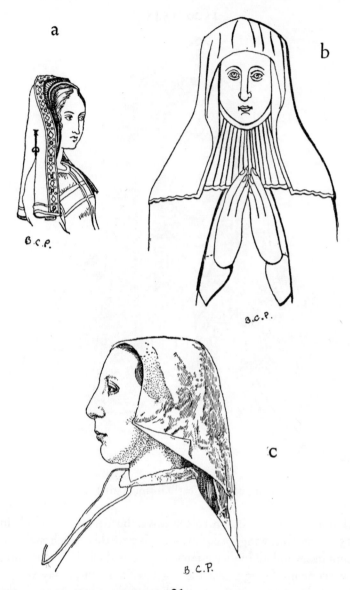

a

b

c

B.C.P.

B.C.P.

B.C.P.

26.

(a) Early draped hood embroidered round the front edge, showing
undercap and hair; also 'clock' at division of 'curtain'. (1500–1510.)
(b) Plain widow's hood and barbe worn below the chin. (1519.)
(c) Plain linen hood stiffened. (1530.)

71

27.
English hood, early form. (1501.)

chin and reaching down to the lower border of the hood. In
1517 the following order was in force: that 'duchesses and
countesses and all higher estates may be barbed above the chin,
everyone not being under the degree of a baroness may wear a
barbe about the chin: and all other gentlewomen beneath the
throatgoyll' (gullet). B.M. MS. Hare 1354 f. 12

A *Wimple* (or gorgette) was similar but unpleated, being a
draped bib carried up round the jaw in front of the ears and
pinned out of sight to the undercap or hair.

'Three lawne gorgettes.' 1589. E.R.O. D/DBR.

(c) *The English Hood*, descriptively called *the Gable or Pediment Head-dress*. (1500–1540, and unfashionably to 1560's.)

The essential feature was the pointed arch which framed the face. This gable shape was maintained by means of wires or a stiffened framework.

The early form of English Hood [1500–1525] was draped, the material hanging in thick folds to the shoulders behind, with the facial border continued into long lappets or *'chaffers'* in front, and usually trimmed with a narrow band of jewelled embroidery set more or less at right angles and attached to the undercap. In addition a broad band of embroidery laid flat across the 'roof' was carried down on either side along the front lappets.

An undercap, generally of white linen, was always worn.

Hair, smooth from a centre parting, was often visible under the gable till 1525.

The later form of English Hood [1525–1540's]. This was more rigid in form, without much drapery. The front lappets were turned up at ear level, and pinned to the crown. The 'curtain' behind was generally replaced by two broad hanging flaps, one or both of which might also be turned up loosely and pinned to the top of the crown. These flaps, when pendant, might reach to below the waist. Above their emergence the back of the hood was sometimes flat and diamond shaped. When all streamers were turned up the whole of the neck became exposed.

Decoration was similar to that of the early style, being confined to the front and crown of the hood. Frequently the jewelled front border was replaced by narrow white, often embroidered, edging from the under-cap.

The stiffened linen undercap, following the shape of the over-hood, often had the lower edge bent up horizontally on either side of the face, level with the lower border of the hood.

It was fastened by a white band or bands under the chin, or left open.

After 1525 the hair was concealed in rolls crossing in the centre. The space under the gable was now invariably filled in by silk sheaths, usually striped and containing tresses of hair turned up from either side and overlapping in the mid line above the forehead. Occasionally the hair was merely spirally bound by ribbon.

(*d*) *The French Hood* (1530–1580, and unfashionably until 1630).

This was a small hood made on a stiff foundation and worn far back. The front border, fitting close round the head, was curved forward on either side to end over the ears, the hair being exposed above this limit only. The back of the crown was raised into a horseshoe-shaped curve over the head.

The curtain behind, of dark material, was arranged in formal pleats, or was merely a broad flap falling to the shoulders. It was often stiffened and turned up so as to lie flat on the top of the crown, with the straight edge projecting slightly over the forehead. Arranged thus it was said to protect the complexion from the sun, and was known as a bongrace.

The bongrace was also a separate article. (See Hood Accessories.)

The English Variation of the French Hood (1525–1558, and latterly always associated with Queen Mary, 1553–1558). The front border was straight, not curved, the top of the crown being flattened across the head, wide of the temples, then turned in at an angle to end over the ears. In other respects there was no difference.

Fastening. The French hood was generally secured by a white, or occasionally dark, band, under the chin.

Under-caps, if present, were concealed.

Accessories to the French Hood

The Bongrace (1530–1615, though mentioned as late as 1636) was also a separate article, made of velvet with a stiffened lining. It was oblong in shape, and worn flat on the head, with one end forming a straight brim over the forehead, the other falling down the back of the head to the shoulders. It was worn with the French hood, or sometimes with a coif, or alone. It protected both face and neck from the sun.

'Her bongrace which she ware, with her French hood, when

28.

English hood, later form, with side lappets turned up exposing the undercap, and back 'tails' hanging loose. Hair in rolls. (1527.)

a

b

29.

(a) French hood. Also shows 'posies of flowers to smell at . . . two or three sticked in their breasts before'. (P. Stubbes) (*c.* 1540.) (b) English variation of French hood. Jewelled upper billiment. (1554.)

she went out always for sun-burning.' 1533. J. Heywood. *A merry play between the Pardoner and Friar.*

The Cornet [1530–1615]. This word originally referred to a hood with a pointed cowl, and then to the prolongation of the point into a pendant flap. In this period it was almost identical with the bongrace, except for some minor difference in shape. The cornet was probably pointed in front.

'Cornette, a fashion of shadow or Boongrace used in old time, and at this day by some old women.' Cotgrave 1611. (See next period.)

'For a French hood xiij *s* . . . for ij coronetts of velvett for my ladye x *s*.' 1550. Lestrange Accounts. 'I never saw my Ladye laye apart Her cornet blacke, in colde nor yet in heate.' 1547. Sonnet by Earl of Surrey.

The Billiment (for the hood) was a decorative border added to the front of the French hood.

The upper billiment adorned the raised curve at the back of the crown.

The nether billiment bordered the lower front curve and to this was often added an edging of crimped cypress.

Billiments were made of silk, satin, or velvet, lined with sarcenet or silk and garnished with pearls or precious stones. Some were made of goldsmith's work only.

'Upper and nether habilments of goldsmith's work for the French hood.' 1541. Letters and Papers. Henry VIII.

The billiment for the head. See Head Ornaments.

Paste [1527–1590] was an embroidered or jewelled border of velvet, lawn or lace, probably mounted on thin pasteboard.

'. . . fine pasted paper such as paste-wives make women's pastes of', 1570. Henry Billingsleys' *Euclid* . . . f. 320.

'Parlettes and pastis garneshed with perle.' 1529. Sir Thomas More. *Supplycacyon of Soulys.*

It was used to decorate French hoods, or worn as a separate head adornment by brides.

(2) HATS, CAPS AND BONNETS (more or less synonymous terms) were far less common than hoods.

30.

(a) Bonnet with halo brim, worn over coif with frontlet. (*c.* 1536.)
(b) Flat cap over under-cap and embroidered frontlet. (*c.* 1532–43.)

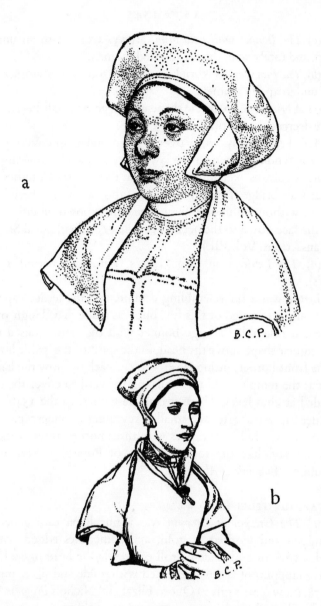

31.
(a) Brimless bonnet, large: wearing undercap and frontlet, and neckerchief on shoulders. (1534.) (b) Brimless bonnet, small; also worn over undercap and frontlet, with neckerchief to shoulders. (c. 1540.)

(a) *The Bonnet with halo brim*, always worn with an under-cap, and rarely with the tilt adopted by men.

(b) *The Flat Cap*, as worn by men, was sometimes worn, with an undercap, by women.

(c) *A brimless Cap*, in the shape of a large or small beret. The size decreased with time. [1520-1560.]

This was usually worn over a large undercap covering the ears, extending down to the jaw, and completely covering the hair. A curious exception occurred in the Eastern Counties and near Cambridge from the 1520's to '30's, when the 'beret' was worn without an undercap and the hair exposed on either side of the face down to the neck. (See Essex Archaeological Society Transactions. Vol. VII.)

(d) *The Lettice Cap* (1500-1580's, but main period 1520-40's).

Lettice was a fur resembling ermine, and the lettice cap was not only composed of this fur, but was made in a design of its own. It resembled a large bonnet with the crown raised to a triangular shape above the head, in the spirit of the 'gable hood'. The front border, fitting close, was cut back to show the hair as far as the temples, and then curving forward to cover the ears, ended at chin level. There was no fastening. In the 1540's the lettice cap was shorter and smaller, revealing an undercap.

'Some weare lattice cappes with three hornes, three corners I should say, like the forked cappes of Popish priests.' 1583. Stubbes, *Anatomie of Abuses*.

(3) VARIOUS OTHER HEAD WEAR

(a) *The Crespin or Creppin* was a fine linen caul generally crimped and worked in gold, and sometimes edged with a gold-work or embroidered roll encircling the head like a fillet. 'Five creppins of lawne garneshed with golde and silver purle.' 1578. New Year's gift to Queen Elizabeth. Nichols *Progresses ... of Q. Elizabeth* (Style 1500 and before, to 1600).

(b) *The Caul* was a close fitting cap covering the ears and usually reticulated in gold thread and decorated with jewels or pearls. It was lined with taffeta, tissue or cloth, and when worn

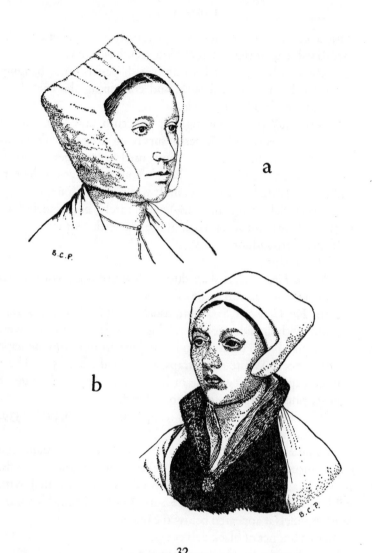

32.

(a) Lettice cap, large. (1527–8.) (b) Lettice cap, smaller; wearing a frontlet. (1541.)

with a crown or coronet was extremely reminiscent of the mediaeval style at the end of the fourteenth century.

In the 1540's the Caul became bag-shaped behind, hanging down to the nape of the neck, and containing the back hair. This was mainly a foreign style.

(c) *The Coif* (worn throughout sixteenth and first half of seventeenth centuries). A term surviving from men's head-wear in the Middle Ages was now used for women's also. It was a close fitting Cap (like a baby's bonnet) covering the ears and generally tied under the chin. It was made of linen (though other materials came into use), and rarely embroidered or trimmed before the second half of the sixteenth century.

It was worn indoors.

(d) *Undercaps*

(i) *For Hoods,* were shaped to the form of hood with which they were worn, and made of linen.

(ii) *For Hats or Caps,* were usually shaped like the *French* hood, with the side-pieces covering the ears continued lower. Some had broad bands bound round the crown from the nape of the neck. White chin straps were usual after 1525. These undercaps might be made of linen or velvet, gold tissue or other fine materials, often embroidered.

'My best whyte (under) cappe and my hatte.' 1539. Rattlesden Wills.

(e) *The Frontlet* (1500 and before,–1600) was an ornamental band worn across the top of the forehead, with bonnets or cauls. It was made of velvet, satin or needlework decorated with gold and jewels, or it might be entirely of goldsmith's work. With bonnets it appeared below the undercap.

'Item a bonnet of black velvet 15s.
Item a frontlet for the same bonnet 12s.'

'Frontlet of green satin with caule of gold.
Frontlet of gold lined with tawney velvet, ditto lined with crimson satin.' 1523. Inventory of Dame Agnes Hungerford.

'One velvet bonet blake with a white frontlet of satten with golde, ii edges of silke womens worke of gold.' 1537. North Country Wills.

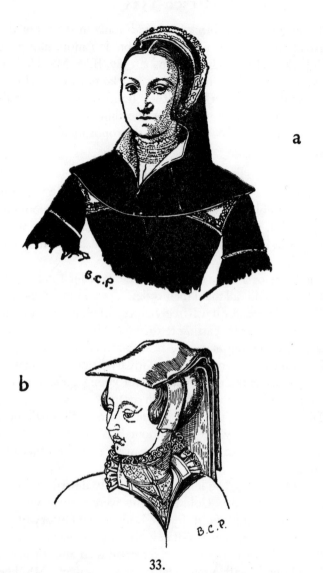

a

b

33.

(a) Tippet. (*c.* 1540.) (See dress accessories.) (b) Bongrace worn over coif. (1530.) (Generally worn with a French hood.)

Mourning Garb was black, and traditional in style. For that of high-ranking ladies see p. 67. 'A surcote is a mourning garment mad[e] lyke a close-bodied gown.' *c.* 1587. B.M. MS. Harl. 1440. f. 15v. The 'slope' or 'mourning cassocke not open before' was still prescribed for lesser ladies; their trains were shorter or absent and their white barbes worn *under* the chin. The mourning hood had a pendant 'tippet' behind, its length proportional to the wearer's rank.

HAIR

The hair was mostly concealed. With the early hoods a minimum was visible, and with the first form of English hood, smooth hair parted in the centre showed under the gable arch. With the second form of English hood, it was concealed in rolls as already described.

'The heare of a woman that is layde over hir forehead, nowe gentylwomen do call them their rolles.' 1548. Elyot, *Bibliotheca.*

With the French hood it was freely exposed, being worn straight and smooth from a centre parting to the ears. After 1540 it was waved.

Long Hair flowing loose, the head adorned with a gold fillet, caul, billiment or wreath, was worn by brides and their attendants, queens at their coronation, and young girls. This fashion continued well into the seventeenth century.

Hair exposed to the neck when worn with small brimless bonnets has already been mentioned as an Eastern Counties fashion between 1520 and '30. The style resembles that of men described under (*b*).

Head Ornaments. The billiment as already described, but worn as a separate accessory. Gold billiments were popular with brides. 'A billiment of gold' worn by the bride in the History of Jack of Newbury. (Temp. Henry VIII described by Deloney, 1596.)

Billiment lace was a gold or silver braid used also for garments. 'jerkine bounde with a billiment lace of . . . silver'. MS. Egerton 2806.

LEG WEAR

STOCKINGS

Long, tailored, and gartered above the knee by

(*a*) A knotted strip of material.

(*b*) A buckled band of material.

SOCKS. 'For ii yerdes of white fustyam for sokkes for the Quene xiij d.' 1502. Privy Purse expenses of Elizabeth of York.

SHOES. As for the men. Boots were not worn.

PATTENS were common.

BUSKINS for riding and travel. 'twoo payre of buskins for the Quenes grace at hure departing into Walys viij s.' 1503. Ibid.

ACCESSORIES

GLOVES. As for the men.

HANDKERCHIEFS. As for the men.

ARTICLES SUSPENDED FROM THE GIRDLE

A 'pair of beads', meaning a string of beads, or rosary.

A Dagger (rare).

A Purse.

A Book of Hours.

A Fur Stole.

A Pomander.

A Fur Stole [1500–1600]. Usually of sable or marten, was lined with silk, and the ends usually tipped with a gold or jewelled mount. It was worn loosely round the neck, or suspended by a chain from the girdle (known abroad as a 'flea-fur').

'To Agnes . . . my furre of grey . . . to my sister my newe furre of shanks.' 1518. Will of a London Grocer's wife. Wayman Wills.

A Pomander [1500–1690] 'derived from the apple (pomme), whence they were named pomme-d'ambre, if affording that scent, and then pomander generically'. Fairholt's *Costume in England*. The term came to be used for the container of the scent ball. A pomander was a receptacle of goldsmith's work, containing perfume and partly used against infection. The shape varied, but was usually a circular flat box, or ball-shaped, with perforations. A variety of scents was used.

The pomander was usually attached in front to the end of the long pendant portion of the girdle. The following is a recipe of the contents: 'Make a pomemaunder under this maner. Take of Lapdanum iii drammes, of the wodde of Aloes one drame, of amber of grece ii drames and a half; of nutmegges, of storax calamite of eche a drame and a halfe; confect all these togyther with Rose-water, and make a ball. And this aforesayd Pomemaunder doth not onely expell contagyous ayre, but also it doth comforte the brayne, as Bartholomew of Montagnaue sayth, and other modernall docters doth afferme the same.' 1542. Andrew Boorde's *Dyetary of Helth*.

'To Elizabeth . . . a gurdell of lowe werke, a pair of beds (beads) of silver, a pomander of silver.' 1520. Wayman Wills.

The Purse, usually in the shape of a small flat bag, the mouth pulled in by tasselled strings. Embroidery and decoration was common.

'A tany bage (tawny bag) with knoppys (tassels)off gold and strynkes (strings) off grene sylke'. 1510. Lincoln Wills.

APRONS, with or without bibs, were worn domestically.
Materials used. Stamin, dowlas, linen. . . .
'My best stamyn apron.' 1539. Rattlesden Wills.

A MUFFLER [1535-1660's]. A kerchief worn over the mouth and chin was rare. See Section II.

JEWELLERY. Pendants, rings, earrings, billiments. (See French hood.) Carcanets were collars of goldsmith's work.

A MOUFLER, MOUFFELIER appears at this time to have been a muff (? from French *'mouffle*, a winter mittaine'. Cotgrave, 1611). The Inventory of Henry VIII's Wardrobe made at his death (1547) included, among women's apparel, two mouflers and a partlet all matching except that one of the mouflers was furred. As both were 'garnished with small perles and small stones of sundrie sorts' they are more likely to have been muffs than mufflers.

1545-1600

MEN

INTRODUCTORY REMARKS

The special features of this period were bombast, small waists, and the increasing use of knitting.

(1) *Bombast* was the padding used for many garments, and parts of them such as sleeves, to produce stiff distended bolstered shapes eliminating folds and creases.

'They shew the swellings of theyr mind in the swellings and plumping out of theyr apparrayle.' Thomas Nash *Christ's Teares over Jerusalem*. 1593.

Bombast consisted of horsehair, flocks, wool, rags, flax, bran or cotton. In Gerard's Herbal, 1597, the cotton plant is called the 'bombast tree'.

(2) *Small Waists* were obtained by tight lacing and tight clothes, but the effect was increased by garments bombasted above and below.

'and gripe their waist within a narrow span'. Hall's Satire VI. Book IV. (1598).

> So slender waist with such an abbot's loyne,
> Did never sober nature sure conjoyne.
>
> 1598. Hall's *Satire VI*, Book III.

(3) *The Introduction of Knitting*. Knitting did not become established in England until the sixteenth century. Although knit wear, particularly knitted caps and gloves, was in use by the nobility at the end of the fifteenth century, this was probably either imported or of foreign workmanship.

87

In the early centuries A.D. the craft was brought to Europe, and became established in France and Italy during the fifteenth century, Paris and Florence being the centres of the great master craftsmen. However, by the middle of the sixteenth century, knitting had taken root in England, and both men and women had learnt to knit.

'Christopher Here sued Joan Matthewe . . . for breach of an agreement for teaching her the art of knitting caps'. 1548. Proceedings of the Hundred Court of Monmouth.

'Item pd by Mary for dyeng and knytting a payr of hosses for Christian 5d. Item the spinning the woole 2d.' 1554. Sir Wm. Petre's Household Accounts. E.R.O. D/DP A94.

After 1560 knitting became a craft of considerable importance, and knitted garments began to be worn by all classes and were much prized. By 1580 knitting had become a domestic employment. In 1580 there was stolen from a hedge (the sixteenth century clothes line) 'a payer of knett sleives being not full finished with the knetting pynnes'. E.R.O. 76/22.

A Stocking Frame was invented in 1589 by an Englishman, and then 'waistcoats and divers other things' on an increasingly large scale were put on the market, and knitting became commercialised.

See James Norbury's paper on 'The Knitter's Craft', in the Journal of the Royal Society of Arts, 26th January, 1951.

THE DOUBLET, still an indispensable garment, was worn over the shirt, or waistcoat if present. It was close-fitting, with a tight waist pointed in front.

The point became sharper and deeper as the waistline (known as the girdlestead) steadily curved downwards.

Round Waists occurred throughout, but were uncommon until 1590, and then usual from 1590–1610.

The Body was padded (bombasted), and generally stiffened with buckram or canvas, with added pasteboard or busks in front. Linings of taffeta or other silks covered the coarser materials.

Extra padding in front was fashionable from 1575–1590, less so from 1590–1600.

34.

Doublet slashed and pinked in design. High standing collar edged with turned-out border wrought in pickadil to support the laced ruff. Skirt, wrists and double wings with similar design. Buttoned down the front; slight peascod belly. Narrow belt and hanger. Small bonnet and feather. (*c.* 1577.)

The Peascod Belly (a Dutch fashion, popular here from 1575 to 1600) was achieved by excessive padding at the point of the waist, producing a bulge which overhung the girdle, and in extreme cases curved down to the fork.

'Their dublettes are noe less monstrous than the reste, for now the fashion is to have them hang downe to the middest of their thighs, beeing so hard-quilted and stuffed, bombasted and sewed, as they can verie hardly either stoupe downe, or decline themselves to the ground, soe styffe and sturdy they stand about them certaine I am there was never any kinde of apparell ever invented that could more disproportion the body of man than these dublets with great bellies, hanging down beneath their pudenda, and stuffed with foure, five or six pound of bombast at the least.' Stubbes, *Anatomie of Abuses.* 1583.

The Neck

(*a*) *A standing collar* [1540–1670], with maximum height [1560–1570] sometimes reaching the ears. This collar was often topped with *pickadils*, which were stiffened tabs, joined and turned out at right angles. The pickadils were partly ornamental and partly useful as a means of support for the smaller ruffs.

After 1570 the collar subsided slightly or remained high behind, curving away in front to make room for the large ruffs of the 1570's, which were worn with a forward tilt, up behind and down in front.

(*b*) A narrow band or a plain round neck with a small V opening in front [1590–1600].

Fastenings of Doublet

Fastened from the top of the collar to the waist by

(*a*) A close row of buttons, loops sometimes replacing button-holes. This was the most usual method.

(*b*) Hooks and eyes, usually invisible, the garment meeting edge to edge. Silver hooks and eyes were used by the nobility, a vast quantity being supplied to Queen Elizabeth. By the end of the century ordinary hooks and eyes cost 1s. a thousand, and this method of fastening was then used by the poorer classes.

(c) Lacing.

(d) United by points (ties).

The Skirt was *short*, and became a mere border, almost hidden by the girdle, from 1575–1585. It was also flared so as to stand out over the bombasted trunk hose, at the same time concealing the points attaching these hose to the doublet.

Variations in the skirt design

(i) Plain.

(ii) 'Wrought in pickadil', i.e. slit into tabs which were sometimes looped; or there might be a scalloped border (commonest between 1550 and 1570).

(iii) Made of separate tabs usually overlapping backwards. The two in front either met edge to edge, forming a point, or they occasionally overlapped, if the cut was diagonal [1590–1640].

The front edges for (i) *and* (ii) might be flush, or separated by a ∧-shaped gap, or from 1555 to 1580 might overlap owing to the diagonal cut.

Double Skirts [1550–1560] were occasionally worn, the upper being shorter than the lower.

Sleeves (Wings almost invariably present. See on.)

(a) Close fitting to wrist, where a short vertical opening was fastened with 8–12 buttons. These sleeves were slightly padded [1545–1650].

(b) 'Trunk sleeves', wide above and narrowing to a closed buttoned wrist. (Cannon-shaped, or sometimes leg-of-mutton style.) Usually pinked or slashed. Frequently worn with sham hanging sleeves, which came into fashion *c.* 1575 [1575–1630].

Very full sleeves such as types (b) and (c) might be used as pockets. 'he took half a pound of bacon out of his sleeve, and two hens and a cock which this examinate did suspect he had stolen.' 1594. Essex County Session Rolls 127/39.

(c) Full to a closed wrist band (bishop style). Sometimes without wings [1575–1600].

Types (b) and (c) were either bombasted, or distended by an undersleeve of fustian or holland, or stiffened with wire, reed or whalebone, and were known as 'farthingale sleeves'.

35.

Doublet pinked and slashed in design, and having peascod belly. Worn with military gorget. Skirt and wings plain and narrow. Ruff and hand ruffs in figure of eight shape. Trunk hose bombasted and paned. Short hair. (1577.)

(*d*) Moderately full above, narrowing to the wrist, but with the front seam buttoned or tied throughout its length, though usually left open in part to expose the full white shirt sleeve [1580's–1600].

Detachable Sleeves (*c*. 1540's on). Any of these sleeves might be detachable, being fastened at the armhole by points or buttons, the join hidden under the wings.

Although doublets had detachable, and therefore inter-changeable, sleeves, they were never worn without sleeves in polite society.

'*Hand sleeves*' was the term used for the wrist portion of a sleeve, and was not a separate item.

Wings [1545–1640] were stiffened welts sewn round the arm-hole to hide the join of sleeve to body. They were necessary for detachable sleeves, but were considered ornamental and almost universally used throughout this period. They were lined with buckram or stiffening, but made of the doublet material, often with additional trimming.

Variations in design, with dates when popular.

(*a*) Plain, narrow and drooping [1545–1550].

(*b*) A flat welt, broad over shoulder and narrowing to armpit, with scalloped or tabbed border, sometimes double [1550–1570].

(*c*) A series of flat looped tabs, a double row being usual [1565–1590].

(*d*) Plain broad projections without divisions. The width dwindled after 1630 [1580–1640].

Rolls (serving the same purpose, though not strictly speaking 'wings'). These were made of rolls of stiffened buckram covered with doublet material and slashed into short sections of equal length. A double row was common [1550–1590].

Doublet Materials were often different from the rest of the costume, though of a harmonising colour. Velvet, taffeta, satin, brocade, were the commoner rich material, while fustian, canvas, rash (inferior silk) and leather were cheaper. Detachable sleeves might vary in colour and material from the doublet body.

Decoration

(*a*) Small vertical slashes, symmetrically arranged on body and sleeves.

(*b*) Pinking.

(*c*) Embroidery.

The Girdle or Waistband

'For a waste band iid.' 1581. Petre Clothing Accounts. This was narrow, and shaped to the curving waistline. It was worn with the doublet, or jerkin when present, but even then might still be retained by the doublet.

Material used. Leather, often embossed when used with hangers for sword, rapier or dagger.

For dress wear, gold, silver, velvet or silk were used, the two last being often embroidered in coloured silks, interspersed with pearls, gems or spangles.

For poor people, *caddis* (a woven tape) was common. 'Item, ii pyeces of grene and yellow caddas for girdelles' [1552–1553]. Feuillerat, *Revels at Court*.

Attachment of Hose to Doublet

Concealed Points [1560–1595]. The doublet lining at waist level, generally reinforced by a canvas band, was studded with pairs of eyelet holes corresponding to similar pairs at the top of the hose. Through these eyelet holes were threaded the points which were hidden beneath the doublet skirt. Thus were the breeches secured.

Visible Points (1595–1630, after which they became mere ornaments sewn on). These were tied on the outside through eyelet holes piercing the doublet body along the waistline, just above the skirt seam.

THE JERKIN OR JACKET, lined, but not generally padded or busked, was worn over the doublet, following its shape throughout the various changes.

The Neck

(*a*) A standing collar, 1540–1590 (cf. doublet) with maximum height in the 1560's, and subsiding towards the 1590's.

(*b*) A narrow band, or more rarely either no collar, or one turned down flat on the shoulders [1590–1620].

36.
Working men in typical long-skirted coats. (a) in the more fashionable trunk hose with 'pullings out' (German fashion). (b) in very old-
fashioned 'tights' (soled hose) with codpiece. (1563.)

37.

Sleeveless jerkin buttoned down the front; long skirt; small ruff. Doublet sleeves finished with hand ruffs. Trunks hose paned and bombasted. Short full cloak. Court bonnet with jewelled hatband and feather. Shoes bluntly pointed with long uppers tabbed, as also the cuffs of the gloves held in the right hand. (1565.)

Fastenings. Secured down the front from the top of the standing collar to the waist by

(*a*) A close row of buttons (commonest).

(*b*) Hooks and eyes, usually hidden.

(*c*) Lacing. 'payd to the taylor for makying of yoelet hooles in the jackets 4d'. 1557. (Extracts from Books of Stationers' Company.)

(*d*) A series of points (ties). 'For a dosen of yealow silke poyntes for William Mekyns blue clothe jerkin 6d.' 1576. E.R.O. D/DP A9G.

(*a*) to (*d*) correspond to the doublet fastenings. The jerkin, however, was frequently *worn open*, fully or partly.

(*e*) One type of jerkin was put on over the head, being buttoned down the chest only. Side openings which were closely fastened secured a good fit. (See Fig. 75d.)

The Skirt

(*a*) Very short, and variously shaped, as for the doublet.

(*b*) Longer, covering the seat and almost hiding the trunk hose.

Sleeves

(*a*) Frequently absent.

'I bequeth to John Turtell my sleveless jacket.' Saffron Walden Wills.

'A common garment daylye used such as we call a jerkin or jackett without sleeves.' 1599. Thynne. *Animadversions.*

(*b*) Fairly close-fitting, and buttoned at the wrist [1545–1650].

(*c*) Loose above, narrowing to a close fit at the wrist, where buttoned along a vertical slit.

(*d*) A short puffed-out shoulder sleeve, with or without a hanging sleeve, real or sham.

(*e*) Hanging sleeves only [1500–1620]. These could be worn normally, the open front seam being closed over the arm by ties or buttons. Thus to wear one and leave the other to hang was the vogue during the 1580's.

Sham hanging sleeves [1560's–1630], were flat strips of material

38.

Sleeveless jerkin with wings. High standing collar with open ruff and band-strings showing. Short skirt flared over very distended trunk hose. Doublet sleeves tabbed at the wrist in 'pickadil', finished with hand ruffs. (1568.)

dangling from the back of the armhole, and having no arm aperture. These vestigial sleeves were added as ornaments, and when in the way were loosely twisted together or tucked into the girdle.

Wings were always present, and similar to those of the doublet.

Materials. Velvet, satin, cloth of silver, russet, frieze, felt, or Spanish leather. 'My jerkin of Spanish leather.' 1567. *The Great Orphan Book* Bristol. The jerkin usually required half a yard more than the doublet, which was cut from three yards, or more if the material was narrow.

Decoration. Embroidered, or trimmed with lace or braid, pinked, paned or slashed (up to one foot or more in length), or chamarré.

Belts were similar to those described for the doublet.

THE LEATHER JERKIN (1545–1575, returning in 1620 in a different style). This was a military garment adopted for civilian use. It was often known as the *Buff Jerkin*, being made of buff or 'spruce', which was ox-hide dressed with oil and given a velvet surface.

Other differentiating features

The Body was cut in narrow panes from chest to waist. The standing collar and yoke were plain or pinked, and the shoulders were padded.

Fastened as for other jerkins, including method (*e*).

The Skirt was short, occasionally double, and usually scalloped or tabbed (wrought in pickadil). It, too, might be paned.

The Sleeves were very short and straight, reaching just below the armpits. These also might be paned. Some had wings only.

'A buff jerkyn garded w^t velvet w^t Buttons of silver and gilt xxs.' 1551. Inventory of Sir Walter Bonham.

THE WAISTCOAT (1485–1625 subsequently assuming a different style), was a padded, waist-length under-doublet, sometimes decorative, often scarlet.

At his execution in 1600 the Earl of Essex wore a 'black sute',

39.
(a) Old man in long fur-edged gown, using hanging sleeve as muff. (1563). (b) Elderly man in long gown with tubular hanging sleeve. Flat cap over coif. (1563.) (c) 'Lieutenant of horse.' Cote with sham hanging sleeve and long skirt. Falling band. Buskins. Spurs. (1588.)

but 'putting off his doublet he was in a Scarlet Wastecoate.'
Stow's *Annals*.

Style without fastening, 'He puts on his armour over his ears like
a waistcoat.' 1591. Breton. *Bower of Delights*.

THE GOWN (1450–1600, subsequently to 1620, largely
ceremonial or professional). Similar in essentials to that of the
previous period, it was worn over the doublet or jerkin, and fell
in ample folds from a fitting yoke.

Length

(*a*) *To the knee* [1450–1570], and was usually worn open,
unconfined by a girdle. It was a fashion (beginning now to
decline) of elegant youth.

(*b*) *To the ankle* [1450–1600], and was also left open, though
often bound at the waist by a belt or narrow sash tied in front.
It was worn by older men, for warmth, ceremonially, or as
négligé (being loose and comfortable) at home, when it was
called a *Nightgown*. Henry VIII had a nightgown of russet velvet.

Neck

(*a*) A deep square falling 'sailor' collar was brought forward
over the shoulders in broad revers, which were continued as a
narrow turned-back edge down the front to the hem.

(*b*) A standing collar, with a step to the narrow turned-back
edge. 'A gown with a standing collar furd throughout with
white lame (lamb) 16s.' City of Exeter Records, No. 26.

Sleeves

(*a*) Long and tubular, with upper opening for the arm, and
usually worn as hanging sleeves, which could be wound round
the hand for warmth.

(*b*) Puffed-out shoulder sleeves, gathered into a band from
which fell a sham hanging sleeve, often reduced to a mere flat
strip of material.

Materials. Velvet, satin, cloth.

Trimming. Velvet guards, braid; fur borders and linings very
common. 'My wedding gown lined with taffeta.' 1569. *The
Great Orphan Book* Bristol.

B.C.P.

40.

Gown faced and lined with fur. Puffed out shoulder sleeves trimmed with aiglets and straight hanging sleeves attached. Decorative jerkin with short front opening. Court bonnet. (1572.)

THE NIGHTGOWN, plain or elegant, was a loose gown worn in the domestic circle for comfort or as a home evening dress. 'A nyght gowne of blak satten furred wth sables XLIs.' 1551. Inventory of Sir Walter Bonham.

THE CLOAK was the height of fashion from 1545–1600. It was said that fine gentlemen required one for morning, one for afternoon, and one for evening wear. It was also retained indoors on formal occasions by older men. Only inferiors went without.

Shape. Circular, cut from three-quarters of a circle or more, it flared out stiffly from the shoulders. Some cloaks had a back or side vents (generally 'guarded'), originally made for wearing on horseback.

Length

(*a*) To the waist (1545–1620, the most fashionable period being between 1580 and 1620).

(*b*) To the fork (average length).

(*c*) To the ankles [1570's on].

Neck

(*a*) *A small turned-down collar*, with or without a step, merging into narrow revers in front and steadily broadening down to the hem [1545–1600].

(*b*) *A standing collar*, either rising from the whole length of the neck border, or from the back portion only, the rest forming a step, the front edge turned back as revers down to the hem [1545–1600].

'I bequithe . . . my nowe clooke (new cloak) last maide wth a standing coller.' 1570. Will of a Merchant. Northern counties.

(*c*) *With no collar or revers.* The broad band of trimming round the hem was continued up the sides and round the neck [1550–1600].

Special Styles

The Sleeved Cloak (commonest 1555–1575) had either puffed out or plain shoulder sleeves, with true or false hanging sleeves, or a wrist length close hanging sleeve.

The neck had a standing collar, with or without a step.

41.
(a) Caped cloak with stand collar and hanging sleeve. (b) Short cloak or gown with hanging sleeve. City flat-cap. 'Pullings out' of hose just showing. (c) Pickadils of cloak collar. Long sleeve with slashed puff. (All 1563.)

42.

(a) French cloak. (b) Hooded cloak. (c) Mandilion worn like a coat with hanging sleeves.

The length was usually to just below the fork.

These cloaks are sometimes difficult to distinguish from short gowns. (See also Dutch Cloak.)

'did buy a black cloak with sleeves.' 1559. Sir Edward Grimston's *Escape from the Bastille.*

Fastenings consisted of cords with tassels of gold, silver or silk, tied as follows:

(*a*) *For cloak worn over both shoulders,* the cords were usually passed back under the armpits and tied under the cloak behind.

(b) *For cloak worn over one shoulder* (1560's on, very common), the cords were passed under the opposite armpit and tied behind, or round the arm, but in either case concealed.

Sleeved Cloaks were very commonly black.

Three Named Styles

(1) *The Spanish Cloak or Cape* [1535–1620], was a cloak with a hood. It was derived from the hooded cloaks used for travelling, but at this time the hood had largely become ornamental. The hood was deep, pointed and usually trimmed with braid and frogs, or loops and buttons, and the cloak itself variously trimmed or guarded. It was very full and short, at first hip length, becoming waist length *c.* 1560. It had a small turn-down collar and step with a turned-back border down to the hem. It might be worn over one or both shoulders.

(2) *The French Cloak*. ('Manteau à la reitre') (1570's–1670's, subsequently a mere wrap). This was long, reaching to below the knees or to the ankles, and was not rigid, though full. It might be 'compass', i.e. circular, or 'half compass'. i.e. semi-circular. It often had a deep shoulder cape reaching to below the elbows. It was generally worn draped over the left shoulder, and was difficult to keep on. It was made and lined with costly materials, and trimmed with guards, braid, lace, and embroidered with bugles, pearls and gems.

(3) *The Dutch Cloak* [1545–1620], was full, short, often waist length, and had wide sleeves. It was always lavishly guarded.

'A duche damaske cloake garded with three guards of velvet and faced with tuftafta.' 1588. Lancashire and Cheshire Wills.

Cloak-bags and *cases* were used for 'clene keping of . . . riche clookys', and were themselves often very elegant. 1536. Wardrobe Accounts of Henry VIII.

Materials and Colours

'Cloakes . . . of dyverse and sundry colours, white, red, tawnie, black, greene, yellowe, russet, purple, violet and infinite other colours—some of cloth, silk, velvet, taffeta, and such like, whereof some be of the Spanish, French and Dutch fashion. Some short, scarcely reaching the gyrdle-stead, or wast, some to the knee, and other some traylinge uppon the ground liker gownes than clokes. The clokes must be garded, laced, and thoroughly faced; and sometimes so lyned as the inner side standeth almost in as much as the outer side; some have sleeves, other some have none; some have hoodes to pull over the head, some have none; some are hanged with points, and tassels of gold, silver or silk, some without all this.' 1583. Stubbes, *Anatomie of Abuses*.

THE TIPPET. A short shoulder cape worn with a cloak or gown. 'A cloke with a vellett (velvet) tippett £16.' 1579. Inventories City of Exeter. Apparel of an Alderman. Henry Shaw, clerk, bequeathed 'his short gowne and a typpytt of black silke which he had lent to Tho. Atkinson for iii dayes to ride on woweinge (wooing) with'. 1595. North Country Wills.

Sarcenet tippets were common in the 1550's, and were sometimes called merely 'sarcenets'.

Stolen from a man 'a sarcenett typett worth 20s.' 1559. Assize File 35/1/7 (Essex).

'I bequeath to Edward Lenthorpe a sarcenet tippettt. . . 1558.' Will of Jennet Arthington. Leeds Wills.

In Edward Underhill's autobiography he states that after a severe attack of the ague he had to wear 'double kercheves about my head' and: 'I muffled me with a *sarcenett* wiche the rude people in the strettes wold murmure att, sayinge "What is he? Dare he not show his face?".' 1553.

OTHER GARMENTS

THE MANDILION (1577–1620, but commonest in 1580's. After 1620 used for livery and referred to as a 'Mandeville'. R. Holme). Originally a military habit, it was a loose hip length jacket with standing collar and hanging 'coat' sleeves (later sham), and wings. The side seams were open, producing a front and back panel. It was buttoned from collar to chest only, and put on over the head. It was frequently worn '*Collie-Westonward*', or awry,

43.

Mandilion worn Colley-Westonwards. Lace-trimmed falling band and cuffs. Hair close curls all over. Small moustache and Marquisetto beard. Scarf over shoulder. (1585–90.)

'Colly Weston' being a Cheshire saying for anything that goes wrong. The garment was thus worn sideways, with the front and back panels draping the shoulders, while one sleeve hung down in front and the other behind. When worn normally the sleeves were often not used, but left to hang at the sides. '. . . the mandilion worn Colley-Westonward, and the short French breeches make a comely vesture that, except it were a dog in a doublet, you shall not see any so disguised as one my countrymen of England'. 1587. Wm. Harrison, *Description of England*.

THE CASSOCK (1530–1660's, off and on) was now a loose hip length jacket, widening towards the hem. It had a narrow standing collar, and full sleeves (i) short—above the elbow, or (ii) long to the wrist. It was a common garment worn by the middle classes (fig. 55a), but could also be elaborate e.g. those of the 'ffawkeners' in the Court Revels, 1554. Feuillerat.

The cassock might be worn under the gown for warmth.

THE GABARDINE (1510–1560, mainly a horseman's coat) was a long loose overcoat worn with or without a girdle, and having wide sleeves. After 1560 it became 'a cloake of Felt, for raynie weather'.

THE COAT still appears to have been a general term for an upper garment, such as the jerkin, or one of looser fit such as mandilion, cassock, or occasionally a gown, but never doublet or waistcoat.

'Their coats and jerkins as they be diverse in colors, so be they diverse in fashions, for some be made with colors, some without; some close to the bodie, some loose, which they cal Mandilians covering the whole body down to the thighe, like bagges or sacks . . . some are buttoned downe the brest, some under the arme, and some down the back; some with flappes over the brest, some without; some with great sleeves, some with small, and some with non at all; some pleated and crested behind and curiouslye gathered; some not so.' 1585. Stubbes, *Anatomie of Abuses* (3rd ed.).

A *Base-Coat* was a plain jerkin with skirts made deeper than usual. It was largely used for livery or military wear. (Fig. 8b.)

'King's pensyoners in harnes . . . and goodly basses of cotes' [at a review of men of armes, 1552]. Diary of Henry Machyn.

The following is a tailor's bill of 1569, 'for a blacke clothe cote.' 'For one yarde one quarter of blacke clothe for a cote at 16s the yarde. 20s.

> For bayes for to lyne the skyrtes.   20s.
> For russett fustian for the upper bodye 14d.
> For sylke   18d.
> For 3 dozen of buttons   9d.
> For canvas for the collar   9d.
> To Busshell for the makyng   3s.'
>
> Petre Archives. E.R.O. D/DP. A9F.

The Shamew [1530's–1590's]. A loose coat worn open. 'My shawmewes, leather doublet. . . .' 1593. Will of John Hunwick of Colchester. E.R.O. T/A 48/2.

NECK WEAR

Throughout this period there was a choice between the plain turned-down collar or *falling band* (band being a general term for collar) and the goffered collar or *ruff*.

(1) THE FALLING BAND OR FALL (1540–1670's varying in shape), arising from the upper border of the neckband of the shirt, was turned down over the standing collar of the doublet. At first small, it gradually increased in depth and became flatter and spreading as the doublet collar diminished in height [1570's–1600]. After 1585 it was often left open at the throat, and became a separate article.

Materials. Usually linen.

Decoration. Embroidery in coloured silks, metal thread or black work very common from 1540–1570's. Elaborate lace borders (1570's on).

A Ruff placed above a falling band was occasionally worn from the 1580's–1615.

> For under that fair ruff so sprucely set
> Appears a fall, a falling-band forsooth.
>
> 1598. John Marston. *The Scourge of Villainy.*

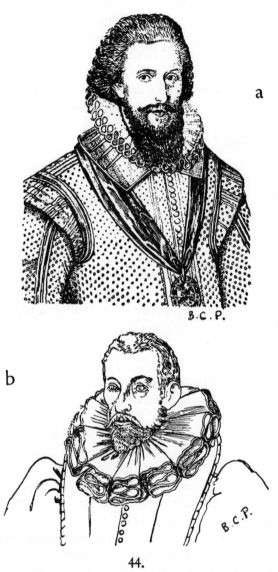

44.

(a) Ruff and Falling Band. Worn together. Hair in the Earl of Essex
style. (1597.) (b) Late Ruff with flattened figure of eight set. (1598.)

(2) THE RUFF (1560's to 1620, and as a falling ruff to 1640). This evolved from the frill edging the top of the standing shirt collar. In the 1560's this frill was starched and goffered, and as towards 1570 it increased in size, the ruff as a separate article soon became necessary.

Band Strings were tasselled ties for fastening the ruff under the chin. One, two or sometimes more, to each side might be used.

Variations in Ruffs

(a) *The Small Ruff*, whether attached to the shirt or separate, was usually worn open in front, with the band strings untied and left dangling or pushed out of sight (1560's–1570's, although small closed and moderate sized ruffs were worn throughout by some men).

(b) *A medium sized Ruff* was generally closed all round, the band strings being tied and concealed (1570's on).

(c) *The Cartwheel Ruff* was immense and worn closed all round, giving the appearance of 'a head on a platter' [1580–1610].

Construction of Ruffs

Ruffs were at first single goffered bands, but later, *c* 1590–1620, they became compound, being arranged in double, treble or more layers.

'They have now newly found out a more monstrous kind of ruffe, of twelve, yea sixteen lengths apiece, set three or four times double, and it is of some fitly called "three steps and a half to the gallows".' 1595. Stubbes, *Anatomie of Abuses* (4th ed.).

The tubular pleats called *sets* were formed by means of setting-sticks, also called poking-sticks or pokers.

Setting-Sticks were made of bone, ivory or wood. Steel pokers were used after 1573. The setting-sticks were heated and applied to the starched material to produce the radiating organ-pipe folds.

Starch for stiffening ruffs was introduced into England from Flanders in the 1560's.

Starch coloured red, blue, purple, green or yellow, is mentioned in contemporary literature, but white, and very rarely yellow, seems to have prevailed in England, judging from portraits.

Starch was a novelty much satirised. 'But if it happen that a shoure of raine catch them, before they can get harbour, then their great ruffes strike sayle, and down they fall as dishcloutes fluttering in the winde.' 1595. Stubbes, *Anatomie of Abuses* (4th ed.).

Arrangement of Sets. This was known as sets being 'ordered' (or disordered, seventeenth century).

Variations

(i) Forming at the edge a vertical figure of eight in one layer [1560–1620].

(ii) Forming a flattened or horizontal figure of eight, often in several layers [1590–1620].

(iii) Arranged in massed convolutions in several layers [1590's–1605].

> *His linnen collar labyrinthian set*
> *Whose thousand double turnings never met.*
>
> [1597–1598.] J. Hall's *Satire VII*, Book III.

Means of Supporting large Ruffs

(i) *The Underpropper or Supportasse* was a wire frame 'whipped over either with gold, thread, silver or silk'. It spread out behind, from the doublet collar to which it was fixed, supporting the ruff which was pinned to it. The ruff was thus given a tilt up at the back and down in front. In the fashionable world, this process of pinning up the ruff to the wearer's satisfaction sometimes took hours to accomplish.

(ii) *The Pickadil*, originally meaning a tabbed border, came to be used for an upright stiffened frame, fixed at the back of the neck and edged with tabs turned out horizontally to support the ruff.

(iii) Pasteboard lining to ruffs was occasionally used.

Materials. Linen, cambric, holland, lawn, lockeram, lace, 'or els of some other the finest cloth that can be got for money, whereof some be a quarter of a yard deep, yea some more'. 1583. Stubbes, *Anatomie of Abuses.*

Trimming. Blackwork, lace in narrow or deep borders, some ruffs being entirely of lace; cut work or drawn work, gold or silver thread, black or coloured silk embroidery. 'His ruffe was of fine lockeram, stitched very fair with Coventry blue.' Robert Greene.

WRIST WEAR

(1) CUFFS, turned back, funnel-shaped, and worn with the falling band, though they might also be worn with the ruff.

(2) HAND RUFFS, made like a small neck ruff, and worn with it.

A Suit of Ruffs indicated a ruff with matching hand ruffs.

A Pair of Ruffs indicated hand ruffs only.

LEG WEAR

This was of two kinds

(1) *Whole Hose* or Long Stocked Hose, consisted of breeches and long tailored stockings sewn together to form a single garment. (1400–1620, but far less common after 1605.) Although the term 'hose' was used to indicate the whole garment, after 1550 it was more frequently applied to the upper or breeches portion. See also pp. 206, 207.

(2) *Breeches*, with separate stockings (1570 on).

The term hose in this category often indicated breeches, and was not finally transferred to stockings alone until *c.* 1660.

WHOLE HOSE
Variations

(1) Early form, with oval expansions starting at the fork (See last section) [1540–1560].

(2) *Trunk Hose* (1550–1610, and, rarely, later), also called trunk slops, trunk breeches, trunks, round hose or French hose. Trunk hose (that is, the breech portion) had two main styles, although many intermediate shapes were also worn.

(*a*) Round like a pumpkin or onion [1555–1570's]. Length about to mid-thigh. Popularly known abroad as 'Spanish kettledrums'.

45.

Trunk hose with Canions. Short full trunk hose matching the cloak.
Canions with a different design. Stockings drawn up over them.
Pantofles worn over shoes with high tongues. Cloak full and collarless, worn over doublet with slight peascod belly and skirt a mere
border. Hair brushed up and pickdevant beard. Court bonnet with
feather. (c. 1575.)

(b) Sloping outwards from the small waist to a maximum swelling below (approximately mid-thigh), then turned directly in to the thigh. (1570's–1610. Rarely, to 1620.) This style was sometimes shortened to a mere pad round the hips by the extra fashionable, from 1575–1600.

Decoration, by paning was, at this period, almost universal, consequently trunk hose were often referred to as '*a pair of panes*,' or merely '*panes*'.

Bright uppermost lining was drawn out through the gaps. 'For one yard of stammell for a payer of breches. For an ell one quarter of chaungeable taffita to drawe them out with, 15s.' 1569. Petre Archives. E.R.O. D/DP A9F.

Nether Stocks of Trunk hose were sometimes ornamented with clocks.

'For sylke for the clockes.' 1569. Petre Archives. E.R.O. D/DP A9F.

(3) *Trunk Hose with Canions* [1570–1615]. Although these were worn with stockings, and might be considered as separate breeches, the design belongs to the genus of 'whole hose'. The upper or trunk portion was shaped to slope out as in style (b), and then ended with canions.

Canions were thigh fitting extensions from the trunk hose to the knee or just below, as if the nether stocks had been cut off at this level. Canions were usually of a different material and colour from the trunk hose to which they were joined, and were always lined, commonly with cotton or fustian to give them 'body'. 'For cotton to line the cannyons and to stiffen them in the bottom iis.' 1581. Petre Archives E.R.O. D/DP A.10. (Some canions were lined with soft material, and then easily creased.) Occasionally they were slashed. 'For sarcenet to laye underneathe the cuttes of the canyons 4s4d.' 1581. E.R.O. D/DP A9G.

Separate Stockings were either pulled up above the knees, over the canions, and then usually cross-gartered (see Fig. 50 (b) and (c)), or else the canions, if wide enough, were fastened over the stockings below the knee. See also p. 126.

Pluderhose (mentioned here because so frequently seen in

B.C.P.

46.
Late type of trunk hose with plain canions. Doublet with slight peascod belly. Wearing a gorget. (*c.* 1595.)

pictures) were mainly a German or Swiss form of trunk hose, worn from mid-century. See Fig. 36a. They were characterised by broad panes with wide gaps bulging with masses of silk or taffeta generally overhanging the panes below. These hose might be knee length or even longer.

The Cod-piece continued to be worn with trunk hose. It diminished in size after 1570, and was discarded by the fashionable world in the 1590's, and by all soon after 1600. The term was used, however, for the front fastening, by humble folk until 1630. But while it was in vogue, 'so little opprobrium attached to this accessory of masculine costume that it served as a pocket in which a gentleman kept his handkerchief and purse, and even oranges, which he would pull out before the ladies' eyes and hand to them.' M. von Boehn's *Modes and Manners in the Sixteenth Century.*

Methods of distending Trunk Hose

(a) With bombast, hair being very widely used.

'For 2 pounds of heare (hair) 18d' (for trunk hose). Petre Archives. 1569. E.R.O. D/DP. A9F.

(b) With several linings, in addition to bombast, usually consisting of two coarse under linings of holland or canvas, and one outer lining of satin or taffeta showing between the panes. A warrant dated 1575 reads:

'For making a payer of round hose of watchet kersey . . . with canyons of carnacon taphata the panes (of the hose) lyned with bayes, [hose] lyned wth lynen, wollen, canvas and heare (hair) with knitt stockinges.' Egerton MS. 2806, f 91

(c) With a padded roll under the lining, and either worn round the waist or hips or lower, when a roll for each leg would be required. The position depended on the shape desired. (Satirised as the male farthingale.)

'For blacke cotton to make a payer of mowldes—2s. For heare (hair) for them 12d.' 1569. Petre Archives. E.R.O. D/DP A9F.

Tyr'd with pinn'd ruffs and fans and partlet strips
And bulks and verdingales about his hips.

1598. J. Hall's *Satire VI*, Book IV.

B.C.P.

47.

Venetians, close fitting. Stockings (with *clocks*) drawn up over them and
gartered above the knee. *Shoe-strings tied in bows* over tongued
uppers. *Doublet* with marked *peascod* belly and 'bishop' sleeves without wings. A buttoned slit in left sleeve used as a *pocket*. Hair long
and pickdevant beard with brushed up moustache. (1583.)

48.

Venetians full, pear-shaped, closed below knees with 'pickadil' border. Sleeveless jerkin with double wings in pickadil. Closed ruff and hand-ruffs to doublet sleeves. High-crowned bonnet with bunch of feathers. (1574.)

Pockets were made for trunk hose, whether ending in canions or nether stocks.

'For making of your slop hose of black velvet being cutt all over canyons and all . . . for ii pockets to set in them.' Petre Archives. 1581. E.R.O. D/DP A.10.

'For 8 sylver lowpe buttons for the pocket holes—8s.' 1561. Petre Archives. E.R.O. D/DP A9F.

BREECHES (with separate stockings)

Styles

(1) *Venetians* (1570–1620, but most popular in 1580's and 90's). They were knee breeches, fastened below the knee with points or buttons.

'And the Venetian hosen, they reach beneath the knee to the gartering place of the legge, where they are tied finely with silke points or some such like, and laid on with rows of lace or gardes.' 1583. Stubbes, *Anatomie of Abuses*.

'For poynting ribbon to sett at ye knee vi d.' 1581. Petre Archives. E.R.O. D/DP A10.

(Venetians, in rare instances, were made as whole hose.)

There were three variations in shape.

(*a*) *Close fitting*, often almost skin tight [1570–1580's]. Stockings were usually drawn up over these and gartered above the knee. Sometimes fastened over the stockings below the knee.

(*b*) *Wide above* and gathered into the waist, sometimes bombasted round the hips and then narrowing towards the knees—pear-shaped [1570–1595].

(*c*) *Voluminous throughout* [1570–1620], with a moderately smooth surface, though after 1610 heavily pleated or gathered from top to bottom.

'. . . Breeches as big as good barrels'. 1568. U. Fulwell. *Like Will to Like*.

(2) *Galligaskins* (1570 to end of seventeenth century). This term was still used for breeches in the early nineteenth century. Also called gaskins, gallyslops, gally breeches, gascoynes or galligascoines. The exact shape is uncertain, but they were

usually wide, though there seems to have been as much variation as in the Venetians, which they probably resembled.

'In their hoose so many fashions as I can not describe, some-
tymes Garragascoynes breached like a Beare.' 1581. Barnabe
Rich, *Farewell to Militarie profession*. But 'their hose sometimes
Spanish like to Shipmen's hose, and sometimes close to the
buttocke like the Venetian galligascoigne'. 1610. S. Rowlands,
Martin Mark-all.

Slops or Slop Hosen, seems to have been a general term for
wide baggy breeches, closed at the knee, e.g. gallyslops or wide
galligaskins; Venetian slops or wide Venetians.

(3) *Open Breeches*, unconfined at the knee (like modern shorts)
and reaching to just below it, was a Dutch fashion from *c.* 1585,
but does not appear to have become an English mode before
1600, lasting till 1610 and reappearing in the 1640's. These
breeches were occasionally slit up at the sides to show the garters
tied above the knee. Usually, however, only the fringed ends
of the bow were visible hanging below the breeches.

Pockets were made for separate breeches.

'For making a payer of blue venetian hosen xviid. For half a
yarde of fustian for the pockettes vid. For ii leather pockettes
for his other hosen vid.' 1581. Petre Archives. E.R.O. D/DP
A.10.

The Cod-piece was discarded with all types of separate
breeches, which were buttoned or tied, the vertical front opening being hidden by folds.

Method of attachment of Breeches. Breeches were fastened to the
doublet or waistcoat by points, as described in the last section.

Points, when visible, were broad strips of ribbon tipped with
aiglets or ornamental metal tags, which were often of very fine
goldsmith's work.

STOCKINGS (often now called nether stocks or nether stockings)

(1) *Tailored Stockings from material cut on the cross*, were made
as separate stockings, but were similar to the netherstocks
forming part of the whole hose. (Used up to 1600, when almost
entirely replaced by knitted stockings.)

49.

Venetians. Voluminous with looped borders in pickadil at knees, jerkin skirt and wings. Jerkin tied by points but open below showing doublet and stray points fastening breeches to the under surface of doublet which has modified trunk sleeves. Hair brushed up from the temples. (1577.)

(2) *Knitted Stockings*. At first knitted by hand, also subsequently by means of the stocking frame (1589). Knitted silk stockings were highly treasured.

Decoration

Clocks [1580's], wedge-shaped with the point upwards, were embroidered in coloured silks or gold and silver thread, and sometimes spangles.

Materials. Wool or wadmol for the poorer people. Silk for the rich, or sometimes leather. 'For two lambes skyns to make a paier of stockinges 16d, for silke to stitche the clockes 2d, for clothe to sole them 2d.' 1570. John Petre's Accounts at the Temple. E.R.O.

Bright colours were popular, and worn by all classes. Yellow was very common, also blue, red, green and violet.

'Then have they nether-stocks to these hosen not of cloth, though never so fine, for that is thought too base, but of jarnsey worsted, crewell, silk, thread and such like, or at least of the finest yarn that can be got, and so curiously knit with open seam down the leg, with quirks and clocks about the ankles, and sometimes interlaced with gold or silver threads, as is wonderful to behold.' Stubbes, *Anatomie of Abuses*, ed. 1595.

Two or sometimes three pairs of stockings were worn at the same time, for warmth.

'Two pair of silk stockings that I put on, being somewhat a raw morning, a peach colour and another.' 1599. B. Jonson, *Every Man of out His Humour* IV. iv.

'. . . besides his ordinarie stockings of silke, he wore under bootes another paire of Woollen or Wosted, with a paire of high linnen boothose. . . .' 1599. Fynes Moryson's *Itinerary*.

SOCKS (presumably worn in addition) are frequently mentioned in wardrobe accounts.

'For fower payer of sockes.' 1569. Petre Archives. E.R.O. D/DP. A9F.

GARTERS

(*a*) *Small Sashes or ornamental bands* of ribbon, taffeta or sarcenet, sometimes trimmed with diamonds, jewels, or gold-

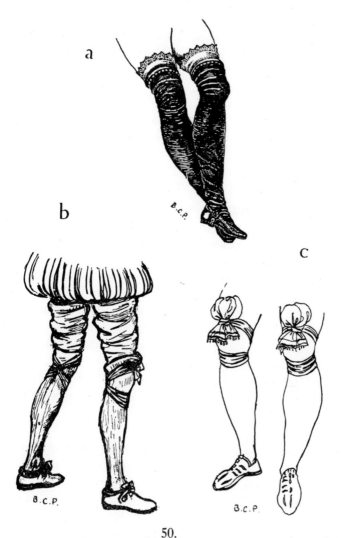

50.

(a) Long close-fitting boots with lace-trimmed boot-hose tops appearing. (*c.* 1595) (b) Cross-gartering. (Back view) (c) Cross-gartering. (Front view).

smith's work, gold borders or fringed ends. (See 'open breeches'.)

Cyprus was common with the middle class. Worsted was used by the poor. Crewell and list were also common.

(*b*) *Plain buckled straps* were worn when covered up and therefore useless for display.

> *What boots it thee,*
> *To shew the rusted buckle that did tie*
> *The garter of thy greatest grandsire's knee?*
>
> [1600–1610.] John Donne

Method of Wearing

(*a*) Usually placed below the knee and tied in a bow on the outer side. Sometimes worn above the knee, especially with canions or with tight fitting Venetians, when the stocking might be pulled up over the breeches above the knee.

(*b*) *Cross-gartering* [fashionable 1560–1610]. The garter was placed below the knee in front; the ends were passed back, given a cross twist behind the knee and then brought forward above the knee, where they were tied in a bow, either in front or at the side. Commonly worn with stockings pulled up over canions. Malvolio went 'cross-gartered, a fashion she detests'. 1601. Shakespeare. *Twelfth Night* II. v. 220.

(*c*) *Hidden* when plain buckled straps were used, and fastened below the knee. The stockings were rolled back over the garters, concealing them entirely.

BOOT HOSE [1535–1680]. *At first* these were inelegant stockings of a practical nature, put on over finer stockings to protect them from damage when worn with boots—or very occasionally shoes.

'For a payer of lynnen botehose 3s. 4d.' 1569. Petre Archives. E.R.O. D/DP. A9F.

Later they became ornamental, being made of finer material, often embroidered or edged with lace round the tops, and sometimes fastened to the breeches by decorative points. 'They have also boot-hose which are to be wondered at; for they be of the finest cloth that may be got . . . yet this is bad enough to wear next their greasy boots.' 1583. Stubbes, *Anatomie of Abuses.*

'For fringe and lace for botehose of russet sylke and sylver ...
15s.' 1576. E.R.O. D/DP. A9G.

'For a quarter of an ounce of golde lace to laye on the toppes of
those bootehose 2s. 6d.' 1590. John Petre's *Accounts*. E.R.O.

FOOTWEAR

General Remarks

Shape. Toes rounded or bluntly pointed [1545–1620].

> *Heels* unraised before 1600, though low 'wedge heels'
> appeared towards the end of the sixteenth century. High
> 'wedge heels' [*c.* 1598] were only worn by the ultra-
> fashionable.

Cork [*c.* 1595] began to be used to thicken soles.

Felt soles were used for tennis shoes (see Section 1).

Material used. Leather—hides of deer, goat, sheep and of cattle
of the bovine species. This last was known as 'neats leather'.

The steere, the hayefer and the calfe, Are all call'd neat. 1611.
Shakespear. *Winter's Tale*, I, ii, 125.

Spanish leather, or cordwain (made originally at Cordova of
goatskins tanned and dressed, but afterwards frequently of split
horse-hides. O.E.D.) was soft and pliable and therefore very
popular. It was imported in large amounts. White leather was
common.

Other materials were silk, brocade, velvet, cloth.

Decoration. Slashing of the uppers was very common, sometimes combined with pinking. Pinking alone was more prevalent
after *c.* 1560.

Construction of shoes. Vamp and heel leather made in one piece
(to 1570).

Vamp and heel leather cut separately, and joined with a side
seam.

Soles were always made separately.

Styles

SHOES

(1) Closed to the ankles, with long uppers, sometimes ending

in two small tongues. The uppers were generally slashed or pinked in a symmetrical design [1540–1575].

(2) Closed to the ankle, with a long upper ending in a small tongue over which straps from the heel leather were tied by

(i) *A point* threaded through eyelets holes in the ankle straps [1575–1600]. Sometimes this join was concealed under the tongue, or more rarely the tie was also threaded through two eyelet holes in the tongue and tied on the outside.

(ii) *Buckles.* 'Payed . . . for 2 payre of buckeled shoes.' 1576. E.R.O. D/DP. A9G.

'For a payer of shoes for Richd Stanley, with buckles. xiiid.' 1580. Petre Archives. Wages & Lyveries. E.R.O. D/DP. A.10.

From 1580 on the gaps at the sides between the heel leather and vamp widened, becoming very open after 1600.

(3) *Pumps* were fairly close-fitting up to the ankle, and had thin soles (one layer) and soft uppers. Being made of clinging material they had no fastenings at first. Towards the end of the century latchets or ribbon ties were introduced.

Set good strings to your beards, new ribbons to your pumps.
      [1593–1594.] *Midsummer Night's Dream*, III. v.

Materials used were cloth, velvet, silk, taffeta and Spanish leather.

Pumps were worn by all classes and both sexes, but tended eventually to become the footwear of servants, and particularly footmen.

'For a payer of calves leather pumpes 8d.

'For a payer of white leather pumpes 14d.' 1569. Petre Archives. E.R.O. D/DP. A9F.

Slippers were probably similar to pumps, and may possibly be represented by a close-fitting shoe with a long narrow tongue, which extended up the front of the ankle. (No fastenings.)

'3 pair of showes and pare of slippers 3s.' 1575. Exeter Records.

(4) *Startups* were country shoes of rough leather, reaching

above the ankle. They were loose fitting, and sometimes called 'bagging shoes'. Fastened by lacing.

> *A payre of startuppes had he on his feete*
> *That lased were up to the small of the legge*
> *Homelie they were, and easier than meete,*
> *And in their soles full many a wooden pegge.*
> *c.* 1570. Thynne(?) *Debate between Pride and Lowliness.*

Also used for sport. 'For a payre of startups to hawke in.' 1569. Petre Archives .E.R.O.

'The term was sometimes applied to the buskin or brodequin made of fine cloth or silk, especially those used in Court Revels.' Linthicum. *Costume in Elizabethan Drama.*

(5) *Brogues* (1586 on) were rough ankle-high shoes of un-dressed leather, the hair worn inside instead of a lining. The uppers were made in one piece, and the sole attached by thongs. Thongs were also used to bind the shoe to the foot. Brogues were only worn by poor people, and sometimes by soldiers.

BUSKINS OR BOOTS fashionable for riding till 1585; fashionable for walking after 1585.

(1) *Long Boots.* These reached to the thigh, but were usually turned down below the knee, thus displaying boot hose or silk stockings. A back slit was often made to aid flexion. The wide tops might be 'faced with velvet', scalloped or tabbed.

These boots, being shaped to the leg, were made of soft stretchable leather, generally well pinked for ease in putting on. They might be fastened by

(*a*) Lacing down the outside from calf to ankle.

(*b*) Buckled similarly. 'For a payer of bootes with 3 buckles a pece, 6s. 8d.' 1569. Petre Archives. E.R.O. D/DP. A9F.

(*c*) Buttoned.

Close fitting stocking-like boots of thin stretchable leather, without fastenings, were worn turned down and then again up, above the knee. These were similar to the dress boots. Lace tops of boot hose appeared above these.

Dress Boots, close fitting, and generally of cream, fawn, or white Spanish leather, well pinked and sometimes also slashed, were occasionally worn with jerkins to match. Both might be perfumed.

(2) *Short Boots*, ending below the knee, were also worn.

OVERSHOES

(1) Pantoffles (also Pantables, Pantacles, etc.). Very common from 1570's on. These had long front uppers only, being similar to mules and occasionally thus called.

'Thair schone of velvet, and thair muillis' [1560–1570]. Sir Richard Maitland Letherington.

The soles were of cork, thickening towards the heel, the height increasing towards the end of the century, more from fashionable exaggeration than from practical use.

Practical Styles were made of stout leather, with soles set with iron or thickened with cork, increasing in depth from toe to heel. They were worn out of doors over boots, shoes or pumps, to raise the wearer from the dirt.

Elegant Styles, which owing to their richness came to be worn also indoors as slippers. They were made of Spanish leather, velvet (black being common), satin, taffeta, scarlet, or cloth of silver, and might be pinked, embroidered, or trimmed with metal lace or spangles. The front uppers and inside soles were always lined with rich material. The uppers (towards the end of the century) were sometimes short, often reduced to a mere toecap, and the cork soles might be raised as much as two inches at the heel.

'And tread on corked stilts a prisoner's pace' [1597–1598]. J. Hall's *Satire VI*. Book IV.

'They have corked shooes . . . and fine pantofles, which bear them up two inches or more from the ground; whereof some be of white leather, some . . . of black velvet, some of white, some of green, raced (slashed) carved, cut, and stitched all over with silk, and laid on with gold, silver and such like. Yet notwithstanding I see not to what good uses the pantoffles do serve, except it be to wear in a private house, or in a man's chamber to keep him warm; but to go abroad in them, as they

are now used, is altogether rather a let or a hindrance to a man than otherwise; for shall he not be fain to knock and spurn at every wall, stone or post to keep them on his feet? . . . and handsome how should they be, when they go flip, flap, up and down in the dirt, casting up mire to the knees of the wearer.'
1595. Stubbes, *Anatomie of Abuses*, 4th ed.

LEATHER PATTENS continued in use.

GALOSHES. As in first half.

'Shoe called Galloge or Patten which hath nothing on the feete but only Latchettes.' 1572. Bossewell, *Armorie*.

GAMASHES. Leggings of cloth, silk or frieze, secured by buttons (1590's).

'No French gowtie-leg with a gamash upon it is so gotchie (swollen) and boystrous.' 1596. Nashe, *Saffron Walden*.

Cockers leggings of leather or high laced boots or possibly both combined. 'His cockers were of cordiwin'. 1593. Drayton, *Eclogues*, IV, 177.

HEAD WEAR

General Remarks

Hats and bonnets were worn indoors on all formal occasions, and at meals up to 1680's. They were also essential for certain dances. Hats were removed in the presence of the sovereign, though undercaps such as coifs might be retained. Out of doors a gentleman would raise his hat as a form of greeting.

'But the nobles . . . they greet each other with bared head an a bow, sometimes gently gripping each other on the outside of the knee. The women, however, are greeted with a kiss as in France.' 1599. Thomas Platter's *Travels in England* (Translation).

Head wear was low and rather flat up to 1570's, but by 1565 the crown began to rise, and by the end of the century tall caps and hats were the fashionable styles.

STYLES

BONNETS OR CAPS

(1) *The Buttoned Cap* continued to be worn unfashionably into the seventeenth century.

a

b

c

51.

(a) Bonnet with full pleated crown and small brim. Small ruff open showing band-strings. Slightly forked square beard. (1563.) (b) the Copotain hat. (1575.) (c) hat with round ('bowler') crown. Marquisetto beard. (Style of 1570's.)

'To my servante a blewe jacket and a buttonde cappe.' 1557. Leeds Wills.

'vi cappes wth flypes (flaps) in ye neke iiiis.' 1571. John Wilkinson, Merchant. Wills and Inventories of the Northern Counties.

'A Sage button cap of the form of a cowshard.' 1592. Nashe, *Pierce Penilesse*.

'A plain old man of three score years with a buttoned cap.' 1608. Robert Armin, *Nest of Ninnies*.

(2) *The Flat Cap* (1535–1570, and as the *City Flat Cap* until the 1630's). As previously described, this was small and round, with a flat beret-shaped crown and narrow brim, turned up or down or straight. Usually a small ostrich tip drooped over one edge, and a jewel or medallion was placed over one temple, on the crown or brim.

The flat cap was balanced on the head, and often worn with a sideways tilt.

After 1570 it was chiefly worn by apprentices, shopkeepers, artisans, and citizens of London, where it became known as the 'City flat-cap'.

The Statute Cap was one made of knitted wool, to be worn by order [1571–1597]. 'By an Act of Parliament of 1571, it was provided that all above the age of six years except the nobility and other persons of degree, should on Sabbath-days and holy-days, wear caps of wool, manufactured in England.' Fairholt's *Costume in England*, Vol. II.

These statute caps were worn by 'citizens, artificers and labourers' for a time, but the law was constantly evaded and the Act was repealed in 1597.

(3) *A small Bonnet with a raised tam-o-shanter-like crown*, pleated into a brim of about equal width with the spread of the crown [1565–1600].

The Crown was sometimes drawn up to greater fulness, and ceased to be flat on the top. *The brim* was always narrow, flat or drooping. Feather optional. Worn tilted, and sometimes perched.

(4) *A Bonnet with a very tall bag-like crown*, stiffened with

a

b

52.

(a) Tall-crowned hat trimmed with buttons. Pickdevant beard and long moustache. (1591.) (b) Tall-crowned bonnet trimmed with buttons and feather. (1575.)

buckram and pleated into a narrow brim. Feather optional; when present set upright often in front from 1580–1595. Worn somewhat perched.

(5) *The Court Bonnet* [1575–1600] was small with a crown gathered into a headband or rolled brim, which was sometimes made of a cable twist of cypress (crape), with a spiral twist of pearls or spangles. The crown was generally trimmed with a small plume and jewelled ornament in front. It was worn with a backward tilt at Court functions.

(6) *The Monmouth Cap* [1580's–1650] appears to have been a tall crowned brimless cap, chiefly worn by sailors, soldiers and Welshmen, once knitted in Monmouth. (See pp. 88 and 193.)

It is frequently mentioned in literature and inventories.
'Item 4 Monmouth cappes at 2s. 4d. a pec.' 1586. A Hatter's Inventory. City of Exeter Records.

The Lichfield Cap (not identified).

HATS

(1) The *Copotain or Sugar-loaf Hat*. 'Copintank', 'copatain' and various other spellings were used. (1560–1610. Very fashionable. Revived as the Sugar-loaf hat 1640's.) Although the 'copyntanke' is mentioned as early as 1508 (Barclay's *Ship of Fools*), it appears that before 1560 it was worn chiefly at Court revels.

The Copotain had a high conical crown, with a brim of varying width, generally moderate, being flat or slightly turned up or rolled up at each side. It was usually made of felt.

'Sometimes they use them (hats) sharpe on the crowne, pearking up like the spere or shaft of a steeple, standyng a quarter of a yard above the crowne of their heads, some more, some lesse, as please the fantasies of their wavering mindes.' 1595. Stubbes, *Anatomie of Abuses*, 4th ed.

> *O fine villain! a silken doublet! a velvet hose!*
> *a scarlet cloak! and a copatain hat!*
> [1596–1597.] *The Taming of the Shrew*, V. i. 69.

After 1585 it was often worn with a backward or sideways tilt.

a

b

53.
(a) Hats with flat crowns and narrow brims. Also shows doublets with low collars and falling bands. (1598.) (b) Hat with flat crown and broad brim; worn over dark coif. Also shows fur stole. (c. 1600.)

(2) *Other Styles*

From 1575–1600 the variations were so numerous that they must be classed together.

Crowns might be high or low, round, or flat topped. A 'bowler' hat style was popular.

Brims might be narrow or wide, rigid or flexible, and were frequently partly turned up.

Materials used for Bonnets and Hats

Beaver (fashionable period 1575–1660, although in use before and after). The crown was often lined with bright material, but the colour of the hat was usually brown, grey, black, white or self-coloured. Beaver hats might be of any of the foregoing shapes. They were very popular and expensive. 'Some of a certain kind of fine hair, these they call bever hats, of twenty, thirty, and forty shillings apiece, fetched from beyond the sea whence a great sort of other vanities do come.' 1595. Stubbes, *Anatomie of Abuses*, 4th ed.

Beaver was not used for bonnets in the ordinary way.

Leather was sometimes used.

Felt was very widely worn.

'Item five littell narrow felts lyned with vellett for men at 4s. 6d. the piece.

Item three braide (broad) Spanish felts after the rate of 16s. the doz.

Item 6 graye felts eidged and banded at 15s. the doz.

Item 10 cullered felts at 2s. a piece.

Item one coullered filt eaten with mothes 1s.' 1586.

Inventory of goods of Gilbert Lymberge of Exeter, Hatter. (City of Exeter Record.)

Although coloured felts were worn, black was the more fashionable.

Thrummed Hats were made of wool or silk woven in such a manner as to give a nap or pile to the surface. Thrummed hats of wool were worn by all classes, but after 1560's tended to become the wear of the lower classes, when the aristocracy took to Spanish felts. See Fig. 74.

Taffeta and various other forms of silk. Taffeta was very popular on account of its lightness.

Velvet

Knitted Wool or *Felted Knitting* was common for bonnets and caps.

Furs, such as *lettice*, resembling ermine and of a whitish-grey colour. This was chiefly used for women's bonnets. *Miniver*: 'The white portion of the fur called "vair" ' (Planché). Vair was the skin of a species of squirrel or of weasel, ranking with ermine and sable. Also chiefly used by women.

Straw, chiefly used by country folk for hats. A 'countryman':

> *A strawen hat he had upon his head*
> *The which his chin was fastened underneath.*

c. 1570. *Debate between Pride and Lowliness.*

Lining used for hats. Taffeta and velvet were the commonest.

Stiffening. Buckram, starch or paper.

'Item 5 steerched hatts of Taffeta at 8s. the piece £2.

4 reames of cap paper att 2s. a ream, 8s.

—quyers of strong cap paper, 2s.' 1586. From a Hatter's Inventory, City of Exeter Records.

Trimming

(*a*) *Hat Bands*

(i) *Crewell* (two-threaded worsted), ribbon, silk cord or cypress. The cypress might be plain or crimped, and was usually given a cable twist and often finished with a bow or rosette in front.

'Item 2 doz & half of cruell bands at 8d the doz.

Item 13 round silk bands at 6s. the doz.

Item 13 playen sypars (cypress) bands at 8s. the doz. 8s. 8d.

Item 18 yeards of currelled sypars at 12d the yd. 32 yeards of smouth sypars at 7d the yd.' 1586. Hatter's Inventory. City of Exeter Records.

(ii) *Gold or silver or copper*, plain or engraved, or made with a cable twist. Pearls or buttons might be used to decorate hat bands, crystal buttons being popular from 1558–1568.

'As well women as men did wear borders of great cristall buttons about their cappes as hat bands, as a worthy garment to distinguish betweene the Gentry and others.' 1592. Stowe's *Annales*.

54.

Hat with high crown trimmed with cypress hat band, jewel and ostrich tips topped with osprey. Large cartwheel ruff. Somewhat long hair and Marquisetto beard. (1586.)

'Hatt of tyffany garnished with 28 buttons of golde of one sorte and eight buttons of another sorte about the band and upp the feather.' 1599. A gift to Queen Elizabeth. Nichols *Progresses . . . of Queen Elizabeth,* III. 446.

'Item one golden band wrought uppon vellett, 8s.

Item one golden band, 6s.

Item 20 copper bands at 6s. the doz.'

1586. Hatter's Inventory. City of Exeter Records.

(*b*) *Jewels,* generally in goldsmith's setting, were placed conspicuously at the base of a feather or elsewhere on the hat. Pearls or diamonds might also be added, singly or in clusters. Spangles or bugles were sometimes added to feathers, or scattered over the crowns of high bonnets, or twisted round the rolled brim of the Court bonnet. '14 thousand bugells 2s. 6d.' Hatter's Inventory for 1586.

(*c*) *Feathers* were popular, chiefly ostrich feathers, as follows: Ostrich tips, plain or topped with osprey.

Ostrich tips topped with three heron's plumes were worn at the side for full dress.

Large ostrich feathers were very fashionable after 1585.

(*d*) *Pinking* in patterns was also used.

UNDERCAPS were worn under the bonnet or hat, and were sometimes referred to as night caps.

Types

(*a*) White linen coifs tied under the chin were worn by lawyers (and in bed).

(*b*) Black coifs and skull-caps, worn by old men.

'A velvet coif, 2s. 6d. a silk coif, 2s.' 1571. Inventory of Ed. Lymet, Merchant. (Records of City of Exeter.)

(*c*) Decorative undercaps. A duke, riding to dine with the Lord Mayor, had:

'Ys (his) hatt and the border of ys night-cappe sett with owtchys (ornament) of perles and stones.' 1557. Diary of Henry Machyn.

THE NIGHT CAP, uncovered (elegant style), 1575 to eighteenth century, had a deep round crown with a close up-turned brim.

'Made in one piece with a lower border embroidered on the reverse side so as to form a turned-up brim, and the upper edge cut in four pointed half-ovals for the quarters of the crown.' Victoria & Albert Museum Catalogue of English Embroidery. John Nevinson.

Materials. Velvet, silk, brocade, fine cloth or linen; all usually elaborately embroidered.

Worn indoors for comfort and relaxation, usually with the nightgown (dressing gown or home evening gown).

Night Cap (simple style). This was made of coarser material, and worn by country men and the poor indoors, and also sometimes out of doors. It was generally given ear flaps.

'. . . . and hath on his hede a white wolen night cappe with two eares most comenly tayde under his chine'. 1581. Essex County Session Rolls.

> *Lolio's side coat is rough pampilian*
> *Gilded with drops that downe the bosome ran,*
> *White cursey hose patched on either knee,*
> *The very embleme of good husbandry,*
> *And a knit night-cap made of coarsest twine,*
> *With two long labels button'd to his chin;*
> *So rides he mounted on the market day.*
>> 1597–1598. Hall's *Satire II*, Book IV.

The Biggin was the night cap worn in bed, and might be plain or knitted.

> *As he whose brow with homely biggen bound*
> *Snores out the watch of night.*
>> 1597. Shakespeare. 2. *King Henry IV*, IV. v. 27.

The term was also used for a child's cap.

HAIR

(1) Close cropped all over. (1545–1600, but more general from 1560–1570.)

(2) Brushed up stiffly from temples and forehead. The moustache was usually brushed up to match. This effect was com-

monly achieved by means of gum. [1570–1600.] The back hair was fairly short.

His haire, French-like on his frighted head. [1597–1598.] Hall's *Satire VI.* Book II.

(3) Close curls all over [1580–1605].

(4) Longer hair reaching to the ears or shoulders, the forehead fringe brushed back from the face to one side, or a wisp or curl left to dangle over the forehead. Occasionally a casual parting was made [1590–1650's].

With this style might be worn a love-lock, which was just coming into fashion.

The Love-lock [1590–1650's] was a tress of hair, grown long and usually curled, and brought forward from the nape of the neck to fall gracefully over the chest.

'A low curl on your head like a Bull, or dangling locke like a Spaniell? . . . Your Love-lockes wreathed with a silken twist, or shaggie to fall on your shoulders.' 1592. Lyly's *Midas* III. ii.

False hair, wigs, hair oil, also patches and paint were used by fops from *c.* 1575.

> *Whenas thine oyled locks smooth platted fall,*
> *Shining like varnish'd pictures on a wall.*
> > [1597–1598.] Hall's *Satire IV*, Book IV.

Face

Beards were the fashion throughout this period.

'There is not so much as he that hath but 40s. by the year, but is as long in the morning to set his beard in order as a godly craftsman would be in looming (weaving) a piece of kersey.'

A great variety of styles appeared from 1560–1640's.

Main Types

(*a*) Vandyke beard—long and pointed [1560–1640].

(*b*) Pickdevant, short and pointed, usually with brushed up moustache [1570–1600].

(*c*) Forked, short and pointed or square [1560–1600].

(*d*) Spade beard cut square and spreading [1570–1605].

This, when long, was known as the Cathedral beard, as it was often worn by clerics.

(e) Marquisetto—cut close to the chin [1570's].

'For xiiii beards marquesotted at xvid the peece.' 1574.

(f) Long and square. Worn by the Earl of Essex, and short-lived as a fashion, but continued with old men [1580's].

(g) A whispy beard or tuft under the lower lip (1580's–1600, revived in 1630).

'the mouse-eaten beard, when the beard groweth but here a tuft and there a tuft.'

'Our varietie of beards, of which some are shaven from the chin, like those of the Turks; not a few cut short, like to the beard of Marquis Otto; some made round, like a rubbing-brush; others with a pique devant (O fine fashion!) or now and then suffered to grow long. . . .'

William Harrison, *Description of England*, 1587.

The Moustache was trimmed with long or short ends being natural except for the brushed up style in 1570's. It was never the fashion to wear a moustache alone.

Whiskers began to be shaved off in the 1590's.

Young men were sometimes clean shaven, but this was exceptional.

Patches were sometimes worn by dandies from 1590.

ACCESSORIES

GLOVES

(a) *Without Gauntlets* [1500–1595]. These were plain with a short slit behind or had ornamental wrist bands of leather or velvet, often tabbed and decorated with points, the hand portion being of finer leather, usually of a contrasting colour. The variation in length of fingers was very slight. The fingers were often slashed to show underlying rings.

> But he must cut his glove to show his pride
> That his trim jewel might be better spy'd.
> > 1597–1598. Hall's *Satire IV*, Book III.

(b) *With Gauntlets* (1590 on).

(i) *Strong*, undecorated, and used for sport.

(ii) *Elegant*, with embroidery confined to the gauntlets, which were open behind, the gap being bridged by several straps with decorative borders (rare before 1600). The embroidery of the late sixteenth-century glove was almost invariably worked on white satin cut out and applied.

The Gauntlets were trimmed with braid and fringes or lace, and always lined.

Elegant gloves were usually carried in the hand or tucked into the belt. Occasionally one might be worn, but rarely both.

Perfumed Gloves, also known as 'washed gloves', or 'sweet gloves', much prized by those of high rank, were imported chiefly from France and Spain (Cordova), the Spanish perfume being permanent. 'For a dozen of washed gloves to give at my wedding 8s. For a dozen unwashed 5s.' 1570. Petre Archives. E.R.O. D/DP. A9F.

After 1580, all types of glove were being made in England. *Materials* used for all types of gloves:

Leather. Cordovan or Spanish leather.

Skins of stags, sheep and horse. Kid (Cheveral) and suede stretchable and very popular. Doe was the commonest. Satin, velvet, silk and knitted silk, and worsted.

'I have sent you . . . a pair of knit jersey gloves.' 1578. The Heyricke Letters. Leicestershire Archaeol. Soc. Trans. vol. 2. (1866).

'For a pair of suede gloves 12/4.' 1570. Petre Archives. D. D/P. A9F.

'In the shop: 2 doz. horse lether gloves and a dozen tand lether gloves 15/.' 1591. Inventory of Gregory Hunt. Records of city of Exeter.

'For a pair of double (lined) gloves of buckes leather to playe at fence with, 3/4.' 1569. Petre Archives. E.R.O. D/DP. A9F.

MITTENS

Continued in use, for warmth.

'He that russleth in his . . . corked slippers, trimme buskins, and warm mittons, is more redy to chyll for colde, than the poore labouryng man.' 1563. *Homilies* II. Excess of Apparel 114 b. O.E.D.

SHOE-HORNS
Necessary for the tight-fitting shoes.
'A showinge horn of iron 6.d.' 1567. City of Exeter Records.

HANDKERCHIEFS
When ornamental in nature were usually carried in the hand; otherwise, in the pocket or doublet sleeve.
'presently putting his hande in his pocket for his handkercher he mist his purse'. 1592. R. Greene, *The Blacke Bookes Messenger*.
Made of lawn, often trimmed with cutwork, and edged with lace or embroidery.
Velvet handkerchiefs were imported from Italy.
Buttons as ornaments were added in the last decade.
'A dozen and six garnishe hankercher buttons, gold and silver 12/.' 1598. City of Exeter Records.
It has been suggested that these buttons were tassel knobs.

MUCKMINDERS
Linen squares used unfashionably either as handkerchiefs or as table napkins.

APRONS worn by tradesmen. Barbers were 'checkerd-apron men'.

SCARVES (1580 onwards)
Rare at this period. When worn for show the scarf was draped round one shoulder; when for warmth, round the neck.
'. . . a russet scarfe about his necke thrice folded under' (a thick ruffe). 1599. Fynes Moryson.

THE BELT OR GIRDLE was narrow, as in the first half of the period, and always shaped to fit the curve of the waist. It was fastened in front with a clasp.

THE PURSE, made of leather, worsted or silk, was drawn in round the top with strings, often tasselled. It was slung from the belt, or carried in the sleeve or trunk hose, but was less used since the introduction of pockets.

'Which made them feel where their purses were, either in sleeve, hose or at girdle.' 1592. Greene's *Conny-catching III*.

One method of making a large purse—'I have a pair of worsted stockens, the legs of them I pray you to get me a purse, a large one, made of them, with a lock ring. I would have the fringe that shall go about it to be of silk.' 1582, The Heyricke Letters. Leicestershire Architectural and Archaeological Society Transactions, Vol. 2. (1866).

PENNERS (pen holders) and Inkhorns were still hung from the belt by those requiring them.

A MILITARY STEEL COLLAR OR GORGET [1560's–1620] was sometimes worn with civilian dress as a symbol of manliness.

THE RAPIER, now largely replacing the sword, was supported from the belt by a hanger of goldsmith's work, or made of an embroidered band.

THE DAGGER (to 1605) was usually slung horizontally behind the right hip by a short chain, or corded to the belt. It might be worn at the same time as the rapier, but was discarded after *c.* 1605.

THE BROAD SWORD was often worn by the middle classes.

WALKING STICKS, often of native wood, were long and generally had decorative metal knobs. Chiefly used by old men.

RIDING CANES, of holly, were plain and short.

ELEGANCIES

Fans were carried by dandies. (See section on Women for description.) 'When a plum'd fan may shade thy chalked face.' 1597. Hall's *Satire IV*, Book IV.

a
b

55. COUNTRYMAN AND HIS WIFE

(a) Cassock and tight Venetians buttoned at the knee over the stockings.
(1587.) (b) Plain loose gown, caught in at the waist by a narrow sash
and worn without a farthingale. Kirtle bodice, sleeves and skirt plain.
Gathered partlet topped by small ruff. 'Bowler' hat worn over undercap. (1587.)

Pocket Mirrors, of polished steel, possibly of glass by the end of the century, were worn in men's hats, or carried by fops and 'comely striplings', who 'weare curl'd periwigs, and chalk their face. And still are poring on their pocket-glasse'. 1597–1598. Hall's *Satire VI*, Book IV.

Masks (1550–end of eighteenth century), covering the whole face, were worn out of doors to conceal identity, occasionally, by men. They were oval and made of silk or velvet, and generally lined. Sometimes they were held in position by an attached button which was gripped by the teeth. (For fuller description see Women.)

Jewellery. Elaborate neck chains, pendants, lockets and miniatures, bracelets, finger and thumb rings, earrings, often as pearl drops; and seed pearls peppered garments and hats. Gems, often sham, were widely used to trim clothes in Court circles.

1545-1600

WOMEN

Though some of the earlier styles persisted, a woman's dress, from now on, was generally made in two parts, consisting of a separate bodice and skirt, the skirt being known as the kirtle or petticoat. The one-piece gown, worn over the bodice and skirt, or over the kirtle only, continued, but was far less important than the gown of the first half of the century, and will therefore be described after the bodice and skirt dress.

The Bodice or body, often referred to as 'a pair of bodies', was rigid and corset-like, being stiffened with stays of wood or whalebone called busks. The centre one was often carved with ornamental designs. These 'stays' were inserted into sheaths in the lining, and tied in with 'busk points'. The waist was low and pointed in front, and often edged with pickadils (tabbed or scalloped) up to 1580. The neck might be high or low. When low it was square until the last decade of the century, when it might be slightly rounded or V-shaped.

The Skirt or Kirtle was the dominating feature of this period, the shape depending on the underlying farthingale, of which there were two main designs, which will be described with the skirts.

'But which is more vain, of whatsoever their petticots be, yet they must have kirtles—for so they call them—of silk, velvet, grograin, taffatie, satin or scarlet, bordered with gards, lace, fringe, and I can not tell what.' 1583. Stubbes, *Anatomie of Abuses*.

BODICE
STYLE (1A) [1545–1590's]

The body, tight-fitting and with a short point to the waist, was fastened down the left side, probably by hooks.

The neck was low or high.

56. DRESS OF STYLE 1A

Bodice tight with low square decolletage. Oversleeves with immense opening for large undersleeves finished with chemise frill. Undersleeves matching forepart which is worn with a Spanish farthingale skirt. Narrow jewelled girdle. French hood with upper and nether billiments. (*c.* 1547.) Forepart and undersleeves gold. The rest red.

57.

Style 1A. Bodice with low square neck and partlet 'fill-in'. Large jewelled wings to bishop sleeves matching the forepart. Spanish farthingale skirt. Narrow chain girdle. Closed lace ruff and hand ruffs. Billiment on the head. Gloves in the right hand. (1575–80.)

Low Neck [1545-1580's] was square and slightly arched over the bosom.

The decolletage might be covered by

(*a*) Jewellery only.

(*b*) The gathered or embroidered high-necked chemise, with standing collar and frill left open at the throat. After 1560 this was usually replaced by the ruff, which might be worn with a high or low necked chemise, the latter again exposing the bosom more or less according to the size of ruff worn (see Neckwear).

(*c*) A Partlet with standing collar, also generally left open revealing the chemise, or sometimes closed. 'For a claspe for Katheryne Petre's partlett 2d.' 1556. E.R.O. D/DP. A9C. The partlet material was often very decorative, and sometimes studded with pearls. It usually matched the hand ruffs or the sleeves and forepart (see skirts), but not the bodice.

(1B) *High Neck* [1545-1595]

This bodice had a standing collar left open at the throat, or a small Medici collar. Both revealed the frilled chemise collar, which was also worn open.

From 1560 the frill might be closed, or replaced by a separate ruff.

After 1570 a closed cartwheel ruff was popular. This bodice was buttoned down the front, or invisibly fastened probably by hooks and eyes.

Sleeves

(*a*) *Funnel-shaped* [1525-1560], with a close fit above, expanding abruptly to a wide opening at the elbow and here finished with a broad turn-back cuff ending at the elbow bend in front, but very pendulous at the back. These cuffs were frequently furred. The undersleeves very full, with lower slashings and a closed wrist with frill from chemise sleeve. (As described in Section 1.)

(*b*) *Close-fitting to the wrist* [1560-1630], usually slightly padded, slashed and puffed and finished with a hand ruff, or rarely with a turned-back cuff.

58.

Style 1A. Bodice with low square neck and partlet 'fill-in'. Standing collar open in front. 'Beret' shoulder sleeves with tight under-sleeves (possibly detachable) to wrist. Spanish farthingale skirt and forepart both with elaborate designs. Jewelled girdle. Jewelled caul on the head. (1560.)

59.

Style 1B. A dark yoke; bodice with high neck and Medici collar.
Partlet with high collar closed by jewelled carcanet. Oversleeves with
wide pendant cuffs and undersleeves trimmed with embroidered bands
and aiglets, which also close the undersleeves at intervals. Spanish
farthingale skirt and plain red satin forepart matching the undersleeves.
Book of Hours suspended from chain girdle. English variety of French
hood. (c. 1545.)

It was varied in any of the following ways.

(i) *With a small round distended shoulder sleeve*, also slashed and puffed.

(ii) *With Wings*
> as slashed rolls, double or single
> as large plain rolls
> as splayed welts surrounding the armhole.

(iii) *With Hanging Sleeves* (and wings in addition), which, after 1560's, were often sham. They usually matched the dress, while the bodice sleeves matched the fore-part.

(c) *A gathered sleeve*, made close-fitting by being drawn in by a series of bands all up the arm.

(d) *A full puffed-out shoulder sleeve*, either round or beret-shaped, with a deep cuff ending above the elbow, below which the sleeve was tight-fitting to the wrist, and of a different material from the upper portion (probably detachable).

(e) *A 'bishop' sleeve*, full from shoulder to wrist, with a tight cuff, and hand ruff.

Wings always present.

The Skirt of the Spanish farthingale type. Occasionally skirts were worn without farthingales, and then hung in folds over under-petticoats.

A Girdle was usual, though not essential. It was narrow, and consisted of a silken cord, a band of ribbon or a chain of gold-smith's work, lined with material. It followed the waistline, curving down to the point in front, whence one end hung verti-cally to a short distance from the hem of the skirt, and frequently terminated with an attached pomander (see Accessories).

A Demiceint, or half girdle, had the front half ornamental, generally of gold or silver, and the back half plain, usually of silk, as worn in the first half of the century.

STYLE (2) [1580–1630]

The Bodice was close-fitting and long-fronted, the depth of the point varying to a certain extent with the grandeur of the dress.

The Neck was low.

Low Neck with stomacher front. The bodice, fitting round the neck behind, had a V-shaped opening in front from the shoulders to the point at the waist. The edges were sometimes embroidered or guarded, or bordered with narrow revers slightly widening upwards and continued round the neck as a flat turned-down collar. This gap was filled in by a Stomacher.

The Stomacher was a long inverted triangular-shaped fill-in for the bodice, and was so placed that its straight upper border produced a low square decolletage in front. The stomacher was stiffened with pasteboard or canvas, and usually busked. It was made of rich material, often matching the sleeves but different from the bodice, and in a contrasting colour. It was elaborately embroidered, or might be studded with jewels and sometimes covered with transparent material to enhance the effect.

Stomacher and bodice were united by concealed ties or pins.

Occasionally the decolletage was eliminated by the wearing of a high-necked chemise surmounted by its own frill or a ruff, and sometimes the chemise, fully gathered in front, fulfilled the function of the stomacher which was omitted.

The Low Neck was finished with any of the following variations in neck wear (see Neck Wear):

(i) A Cartwheel Ruff.

(ii) A Fan-shaped Ruff.

(iii) A Rebato (p. 168).

The last two were generally reserved for unmarried women. *Girdle* optional. A small sash tied in front was common.

Sleeves

(a) *Bombasted 'bishop' sleeves* with wings and hand ruffs [1575–1585].

(b) *Trunk Sleeves*, full, or very full, above, and tapering to a fitting wrist, were sometimes described as demi-cannon sleeves [1575–1620].

'What's this? A sleeve? 'tis like a demi-cannon.' 1596–1597. Shakespeare. *Taming of the Shrew*, IV. iii. This sleeve was rigidly distended with buckram, reed, wire or whale-bone set in a lining of fustian or holland. Such sleeves were consequently often called 'farthingale sleeves'.

60.

Style 2. Bodice with long stomacher front dipping to a point in front over the frounced French farthingale skirt. Trunk sleeves with cuffs and immense hanging sleeves behind. Laced fan-shaped ruff, and behind a wired head rail trimmed with jewels. Pearls in the hair and jewelled head ornament. Folding fan in right hand, and gloves with tabbed cuffs in the left. (1592.)

61.
Style 2. Deep pointed bodice with gathered chemise replacing the stomacher. Small closed ruff and hand ruffs to trunk sleeves. Small French farthingale skirt with embroidered forepart. French hood in English style. (*c.* 1597.)

'Such lace as shall be requisite for . . . and furdinall (farthingale) sleeves.' 1592. From a Shrewsbury tradesman's invoice to Sir W. Morris. Trunk sleeves were pinked or slashed in designs, or trimmed with lace or embroidery. Some were puckered in a shallow honeycomb pattern, very frequently seen in effigies.

Trunk sleeves were worn with either wings, or rolls, or with immense flowing hanging sleeves, usually sham.

Cuffs at the wrist were usual. Occasionally cuff and hand ruff were worn together.

The Skirt, usually of the French farthingale shape, but either style, French or Spanish, was permissible.

In the 1590's the skirt was often hitched up in the 'dairy-maid' manner to show the elegant underskirt, especially in the absence of a farthingale.

FARTHINGALES [1545–1620's] were not invariably worn but, once introduced, the Spanish farthingale [1545–1600] spread rapidly to all classes.

The French farthingale [1580–1620] was more exclusive. Farthingales vanished in the 1620's.

(1) *The Spanish Farthingale*, also called Verdingale. (1545–1600, but less popular after 1590.) It was an underskirt distended by circular hoops made of rushes (called 'bents'), wood, wire, or whalebone. Each hoop increased in circumference from above down, reaching a wide circle at the feet. The arrangement varied slightly, producing a funnel, a dome or a bell-shaped skirt, the funnel being the commonest. Some farthingales had a single hoop at the hem only.

Materials used were mockado, fustian, buckram, and all kinds of woollen stuffs; also expensive materials of silk weave, including velvet. 'For taking asunder of a farthingale of white satten the forepart new satten and bottomed wt. vellat and bent.' 1572. B.M. MS. Egerton 2806.

What pride can the pore verdynalles increased in women kynde,
The stuf that goeth to the same is easy for to fynde,
Is fustian, or buckram, lystes and eke red cloth.

Utterson's *Early Popular Poetry.*

Farthingales were also lined.

'Item for the lynyng and mendyng of 2 vardgales—14d.' 1555. Petre Archives. E.R.O. D/DP. A9A.

The Spanish Farthingale Skirt. This skirt was gored so as to slope stiffly outwards from waist to ground, presenting a smooth flat surface without folds. When present these were evenly arranged, avoiding any drapery effects. This was known as a 'round kirtle', as opposed to the trained kirtle.

Trains were rare, and only used at

(i) Court functions.

(ii) Weddings or Funerals.

(iii) Ceremonial occasions.

Kirtles were always lined.

'For 6 yardes white satten for a *trayne Kirtle* at 10s. 8d. the yarde. . . .

'For 1¾ ell (ell—1¼ yds.) of white taffetay sarcenet to lyne the trayne of the white satten kirtle at 8s. the ell. For 3 ells of blacke Englishe worsted, and 3¼ for a *rounde Kirtle* and a cassocke at 13s. the ell. . . . For 3 yardes redd cotton to lyne a crymsyn satten kirtle at 12d. the yarde . . . 3s.' 1559. Petre Family Accounts. Money disbursed in preparation for a wedding. E.R.O. D/DP A9D.

'One reed (red) Sattan damaske kirtle wth a traine XXs.' 1568. Will of Katherine Lady Hedworth.

A ∧-shaped opening in front was common, the space being filled in by an elegant under-petticoat, or by a *forepart*.

A Forepart was the exposed front part of an otherwise plain underskirt, whether kirtle or Spanish farthingale. The forepart was lavishly decorated, embroidered, pinked, furred, or trimmed with lace, spangles or oes. It contrasted with the skirt, but often matched the sleeves.

(2) *The French Farthingale* [1580–1620's], mentioned in Queen Elizabeth's Accounts as early as 1561, the 'Wheel' variety being worn at Court in the 1560's. But this was a limited exclusive fashion.

There were two main styles, both producing a tub-shaped hang to the skirt.

(*a*) *The Roll Farthingale*, popularly known as the 'Bum Roll', was a padded roll, variously covered with cotton or other bombast, and sometimes wired or whale-boned.

'One roole covered with Karnacion rybben. One Roole covered with whight tape.' 1589. E.R.O. D/DBa.

It resembled a life-belt with a break in front where it was tied by tapes. It was worn round the hips with a slight tilt up behind and down in front.

'A boulster for their Buttockes.' 1600. Samuel Rowlands, *Satyre VII.*

The Demi- or Semi-circled Farthingale [1580–1620], was a variation, made as a half roll, somewhat resembling a large bustle, and leaving a straight front.

Roll farthingales, by the end of the century were becoming plebeian.

'Nor you nor your house were so much as spoken of before I debased myself from my hood and my farthingale, to those bum rolls. . . .' 1601. Ben Jonson, *The Poetaster.*

(*b*) *The Wheel Farthingale* [1580–1620's]. Also called the 'Catherine wheel Farthingale', and by some the 'Italian Farthingale'. This was a wheel-shaped structure made of wire or whalebone, covered with material such as silk or damask. It was worn round the waist with a slight tilt forward, up behind and down in front. This tilt was enormously increased at the turn of the century.

The skirt was carried out at right angles to a width varying from eight to forty-eight inches before falling vertically to the feet.

'For making sixe Varthingalles of tafata wth wyer and silke to them. For making six Varthingalls of damaske with wyer and silke to them.' 1612–1613. Warrant to the Great Wardrobe on the Princess Elizabeth's Marriage.

> *Alas poore verdingales must lie in the street,*
> *To house them no dore in the citie made meet,*
> *Since at our narrow doores they in cannot win.*

1599. Heywood, *Micro-Cynicon—Sixe Snarling Satyres.*

(c) *The Scotch Farthingale* (unidentified) was in all probability a small edition of the roll or wheel.

'Enter Poldavy, a French tailor, with a Scottish farthingale ... "Tailor Poldavy, prithee fit, fit it. Is this a right Scot? Does it clip close and bear up round?"' 1605. Chapman, Jonson and Marston, *Eastward Hoe.*

Method of tilting the Farthingale (down in front and up at the back). A cushion, known as a '*Cushionet*' was probably worn as a bustle to push up the structure behind.

'A varinngale and quissionet of fustion in Ap^res, iis.' 1566. Will of Wm. Claxton of Burnehall.

The French Farthingale Skirt. The skirt was gathered and made full enough to be carried out horizontally over the farthingale, and then to fall vertically to the feet, producing a tub-shaped outline. Modified, the skirt was worn over the semi-circled farthingale, or with the exaggerated tilt, towards 1600. A Λ-shaped opening in front, occasionally a mere slit, would reveal a forepart or underskirt, but this was far less common than with the Spanish farthingale style.

Trains, when worn, were rare with this type of skirt.

The frounced skirt [1590–1630]. To avoid the hard line made by the wheel farthingale, the skirt was given a circular frill of its own material. This resembled an immense ruff worn round the waist, the sets radiating horizontally to the edge of the farthingale.

These flounces varied slightly in design.

THE GOWN. An overgarment for warmth or formal occasions was worn over the bodice and skirt.

Style (1). *Loose-Bodied* [1545–1620's]. Fitting the shoulders, it fell in set folds, spreading outwards to the ground, often leaving a Λ-shaped opening in front from neck to hem, revealing the dress beneath. It was untrained unless ceremonial.

The Neck

(a) A standing collar with rounded corners, tied or buttoned in front, or left open.

62.

Loose-bodied gown with high neck surmounted by small ruff; fastened by ribbon ties down to the front. Borders edged with fur. Puffed-out shoulder sleeves with jewelled under-sleeves and hand ruffs. Vertical slits at breast level. Is wearing a French hood and holding gloves with short cuffs, in left hand. (1560–65.)

a

b

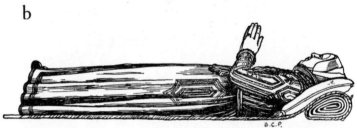

63.

(a) Loose-bodied gown worn with fur stole which is without gilt
finials. (b) The same showing fitchet opening on the left side; narrow
sash closing the gown at the waist; sleeves puffed out at the shoulder.
(1572–80.)

(*b*) A flat rounded collar continued forward as narrow revers down to the hem.

(*c*) A small round turn-over collar.

Fastening. Although usually worn open, buttons and loops or ties might be provided, edging the front borders, closing the gown from neck to waist or neck to hem. A narrow sash sometimes fastened the gown at the waist.

Sleeves

(*a*) Short, puffed out, often with a kick-up at the shoulder, they ended above the elbow, where they were gathered or shaped into a band. The fulness above left room for the wings of the undersleeve. Worn with or without hanging sleeves, true or false.

(*b*) Wings and long tubular hanging sleeves with large diamond-shaped openings at elbow level.

(*c*) No sleeves, but wings as rolls, or welts, tabbed or wrought in pickadil, often in several layers.

Style (2) *The Close-bodied Gown* [1545–*c*. 1640's].

Fitting the figure to the waist and expanding over the hips, the gathered skirt fell in stiff folds to the ground. (Variations in fit occurred, and some were made loose at the back.)

The Neck

(i) A small round turn-over collar was usual. The ruff appeared above this.

(ii) A standing collar.

(iii) A high Medici collar.

The gown was open in front but might be fastened from neck to hem, or from neck to waist (usual), the skirt falling apart leaving a Λ-shaped gap.

Fastened by a series of ribbon bows, which when not in use were tied in loops and used for decoration. Buttons and loops were sometimes used.

Fitchets were vertical placket holes occasionally present, and placed at hip level. Through these, articles suspended from the girdle could be reached if the gown were closed.

Sleeves (Wings might or might not be present.)

a

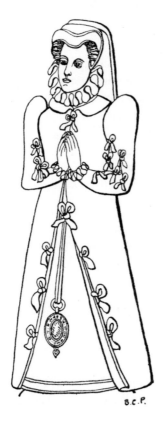

b

64.

(a) Close-bodied gown with small turn-over collar. Fastened by ribbon ties down to waist level only. Trunk sleeves decorated by ribbon bows. Pomander slung from kirtle belt (hidden beneath the gown). Mary Stuart hood. (1577.) (b) Close-bodied gown with high Medici collar surmounted by the standing collar of the partlet. Puffed-out shoulder sleeves and close under-sleeves. Pomander and Stuart hood. (1570.)

(a) A puffed-out shoulder sleeve, gathered or shaped into a broad band round the upper arm, and continued with a close-fitting sleeve to the wrist, finished with a hand ruff. This lower sleeve might belong to an under-bodice, or was a detachable sleeve. A long sham hanging sleeve was usually attached to the upper short sleeve.

'Hir gowne was of black sattin painted, with a trayne (i.e. ceremonial) and long sleeves to the grownde (hanging sleeves) sett with acorne buttons of jett trymmed with pearle, and shorte sleeves of sattyn black, cutt, with a payre of sleeves of purple velvet whole under them (detachable sleeves)'. 1587. Letter to Sir William Cecil—the execution of the Queen of Scots.

(b) Cannon or trunk sleeves (less usual).
Decoration of gowns (1) *and* (2).
Broad guards of velvet or braid or fur. Ribbon, loops and buttons.

A *vertical slit* down each breast to the waist, made to button up, was occasionally added. Whether for ornament, such as a slash, or for adjusting the fit, is uncertain.

N.B. A looser, unwaisted variation was occasionally worn by older women. It was in other respects similar.

The Night Gown was a home evening gown or négligé.

The Bedgown was, in modern terms, a dressing gown. A true nightdress was a 'night-smock'. (See New Year Gifts to Q. Mary, 1556, in Nichols' *Manners & Expences* . . . .

DRESS ACCESSORIES

Neck Wear

(a) The frill, or small ruff, attached to the high collar of the chemise was worn up to 1560, and less often to 1580. Usually left open [1555–1570], though it might be closed after 1560.

(b) *The Separate Ruff* [1560's–1630's]. This resembled that used by men and was worn with a high-necked bodice, a high-necked partlet, or a chemise fill-in. Ruff and bodice were left open at the throat [1555–1570's].

(c) *The Cartwheel Ruff* [1580–1610], and those of intermediate sizes [1570–1630] might be worn with high- or low-necked bodices thus

(i) Closed all round, the band strings concealed.

(ii) Tied under the chin, and the front edges allowed to fall apart leaving a ∧ opening exposing the bosom of a low-necked bodice.

(d) *The Fan-shaped Ruff* (1570–1625, but had occurred as early as 1550). Worn with a low-necked bodice, the ruff rose from the sides and back of the decolletage, spreading out fan-wise behind the head. This style was largely reserved for ceremonial occasions, and generally worn by unmarried women.

(e) *The Rebato or Wired Collar* [1580–1635]. This was a shaped collar, wired to stand up round the back of the head from the egde of the low-necked bodice to which it was pinned, similarly to the fan-shaped ruff. It was usually trimmed and edged with lace, and sometimes made up of several layers.

'Three rebateres of whight loomeworke

Two rebateres of single cutt worke

Rebating wiers.' 1589. E.R.O. D/D. Ba.

'I see Gentlewomen . . . burning out many pounds of candle in pinning their treble rebaters.' 1593. Nashe's *Christ's Tears over Jerusalem.*

For Construction of Ruffs, Means of supporting Ruffs and Rebatos, Materials and trimming, see section on Men.

N.B. Coloured starch was probably less rare with women than with men, and perhaps commoner than supposed among the class that did not have their portraits painted.

'Now the womenfolk of England who have mostly blue grey eyes, and are fair and pretty . . . lay great store by ruffs and starch them blue so that their complexion shall appear the whiter.' 1599. Thomas Platter's *Travels in England* (Translation).

Blue pother starch was 2s. 1d. a pound, White starch was 2d. a pound. (Linthicum.)

Falling Bands corresponding to those worn by men, with cuffs to match, were worn in France, but do not appear to have been an English fashion in the sixteenth century, judging by portraits. On the other hand we have the following entry in a list of linen

65.

Mary Stuart hood and wired head rail flowing to the ground; probably made of cobweb lawn. Open lace ruff. Bodice of style 1A, with plain close-sleeves. (1578.)

for Susan Barrington 'Two lawne bandes, Two Cambrick bandes'. 1589. E.R.O. D/D Ba.

Wrist Wear

(a) *Hand Ruffs* (Ruffles in the seventeenth century) [1555–1630]. Made like small wrist ruffs, were worn with neck ruffs.

(b) *Turned-back cuffs* (c. 1580 on). Came in as an alternative wrist wear, and were worn with ruffs or rebatos.

Materials, such as lace, lawn, cambric, were similar to those

169

of ruffs. Embroidery in black wool or coloured silk was popular. Typical of several New Year gifts to Queen Mary in 1556 was 'a partlett and a peire of ruffes, wrought with golde and blewe silke.' Nichols. *Manners & Expences* . . .

The Rail continued. It was often in the form of a large diaphanous shawl.

The Night Rail continued. Both became more decorative, with lace trimmings.

The Head Rail became very elaborate, and much larger, and was sometimes starched.

'For mendinge, washinge and starchinge of a heade raille of fine white sipers (cobweb-lawn) edged rounde aboute with white thred bone lace.' 1588. B.M. MS. Egerton 2806 f. 233.

The Wired Head Rail [1590–1620] was threaded with wire to form an arch over the head, the rest flowing over the shoulders. The arch might be bent into fanciful shapes, such as a trefoil, the centre leaf curving over the head, or might be left merely as a high collar spreading round the back of the head. It was usually made of some diaphanous material, and edged with lace to which was often added pearls, jewels, gold or silver oes.

'On hir head shee had a dressing of lawne edged with bone lace (a Marie Stuart hood). . . . A Vale of lawne fastened to hir caule bowed out with wyer, and edged round about with boane lace.' 1587. Narrative of the execution of the Queen of Scots, in a letter to the Right Hon. Sir William Cecil.

OTHER GARMENTS

THE DOUBLET was a padded bodice worn instead of the kirtle bodice if desired. It followed the lines of the male doublet, except for the peascod belly. (This was occasionally seen abroad.) The long pointed front continued until about 1615, but a round waist and hem appeared towards 1600. Sleeves were straight and winged. The doublet was lined with canvas and taffeta or similar materials, and fastened with buttons, or hooks and eyes. In many cases it was indistinguishable from an ordinary bodice. The under-petticoat was sometimes tied to a doublet of simple design.

Embroidery with an all-over pattern was usual at the end of the century.

> *Some women a doublet of fyne linnen use to weare*
> *Unto which they tye theyr nether geare.*
> 1566. Lewis Wager. *Repentance of Mary Magdalene.*

'The women also have dublets . . . buttoned up the brest, and made with wings, welts and pinions on the shoulder points, as men's apparel is for all the world.' 1583. Stubbes, *Anatomie of Abuses.*

THE WAISTCOAT, OR JACKET, similar to that of the men, was worn for warmth. 'A wastcote of white lynen, quylted.' 1556. *New Year's Gifts to Queen Mary* in Nichols. *Manners & Expences...*
'An old smock and a wastecote 12d.' 1590. Belonging to the sister of Hugh Bedwell, Shoemaker. Records of the City of Exeter.

OUTER GARMENTS

THE CLOAK was largely a wrap in the form of a long cape, used for travelling.
'Some have capes reaching down to the midst of their backs, faced with velvet or else with some fine wrought taffetie, at least, fringed about, very bravely.' 1583. Stubbes, *Anatomie of Abuses.*

THE SAFEGUARD (mentioned in 1546 but common from 1570's–1630's) was a skirt, worn over the kirtle for protection against dirt when riding, or for warmth when travelling. It is frequently listed with the Cloak. 'I bought . . . a clock (cloak) and a save-guard of cloth laced with black lace to keep me warm on my journey.' 1616. Diary of Lady Anne Clifford.

THE LAPMANTLE was a blanket or rug to put over the knees, serving a similar purpose to the safeguard. Lapmantles are listed in Queen Elizabeth's Wardrobe, 1600. (Nichols. *Progresses* . . II.)

THE JUPPE was a riding coat generally matching the safeguard. 'A safegard with a jhup or gaskyn coate of faire satten' Ibid. III, 3.

THE COAT, often mentioned in middle class wills, was a jacket.

'Also I give . . . one shorte Gowne to make her a cote of. Also to her sister . . . one violet jacket, and to Jennet Duckworth one marble (see Glossary) jacket to make her a cote of.' 1559. Will of Ed. Wood. Leeds Wills.

'My workdaye coytt.' 1556. Will of Ellen Dawson. Leeds Wills.

'By the masse chil (I will) rather spend the cote that is on my backe...' 1575. *Gammer Gurton's Needle*.

THE FROCK was probably a loose gown.

'I will that Frances . . . have my frocke and Elizabeth . . . my best gowne.' 1561–1562. Will of Janet Cowper of Leeds. Leeds Wills.

THE CASSOCK [1545–1580's], appears to have been a gown made 'cassock-wise', i.e. similar to the garment described for men. It probably resembled the coat, but had loose open sleeves, and was sometimes provided with a hood. It was fastened by hooks.

'Item poynting ribbone for mistres Dorothes cassocke 12 yardes after 2½d. the yard, 2s. 6d. Item thredde and hookes for the same cassocke—4d.' 1555. E.R.O. D/DP. A9A.

THE GABARDINE was similar to that worn by men.

'I bequeath to Alice Hartley my gaberdyn.' 1557. Leeds Wills.

HEAD WEAR

(1) THE FRENCH HOOD. (1530–1590, and lingered unfashionably until *c.* 1630.) This continued as described in the previous section, but the stiffened falling fold behind became narrower. It was often turned up so as to lie flat on the head with the lower border forming a straight brim above the forehead. In this position it was, as formerly, known as a 'bongrace'.

(2) THE MARY STUART HOOD [1550–1630]. (The hood associated with the portraits of Mary, Queen of Scots.) This was a small hood of lawn, linen or similar material, generally trimmed with insertion and edged with lace. The front border was wired so as to form a wide curve with a dip above the centre of the forehead, varying from a sharp angle to an open

U. This was the characteristic feature. The sides were brought forward, ending over the ears, and the hair was visible at the temples. A pendant tail behind was optional. When present it was usually of gathered lawn, and commonly worn by widows.

The Dutch often covered the hair with an under-cap of lace.

Change in Shape [1590's–1630]. The hood grew larger. The front border had a wide spread, and was turned back at right angles, the dip over the forehead persisting throughout. The front border was usually trimmed with lace (in a vandyke pattern), which was also frequently set upright round the back of the crown.

Modified *Mary Stuart Hoods* were worn for mourning, and by widows. See p. 67.

Hood Accessories

The *Bongrace* and *Cornet* [1530–1615], as described in Section I, continued to be worn with the French or Mary Stuart Hoods.

'A cornet 4s. 8. a bonnegrace 4s.' 1559. From a Trousseau List. E.R.O. D/DP. A9D.

The *Shadow* [1580–1605] was a bongrace made of linen, lace, lawn, cypress or net-work, and trimmed with lace. This became more popular than the velvet bongrace.

'Five shadowes edged with lace.' 1589. E.R.O. D/D. Ba.

The *Billiment* for the French Hood continued in use.

Paste as in Section I. 'Item 2 hoode pasteis 12d.' 1555. E.R.O. D/DP. A9A.

HATS AND BONNETS were usually, though not always, kept for riding, travelling or country wear. They corresponded within limits to those worn by men, but were generally smaller, and less often worn with a sideways tilt. They were worn over a reticulated caul or linen cap.

Women's hats became much commoner after 1600.

(1) BONNETS AND CAPS

(*a*) The '*Taffeta Pipkin*', a popular term [1565–1595]. (See Style (3) for men.) This had a moderately deep full crown pleated into a head band; the brim was narrow, flat, drooping or slightly curved hood-wise, and the bonnet was

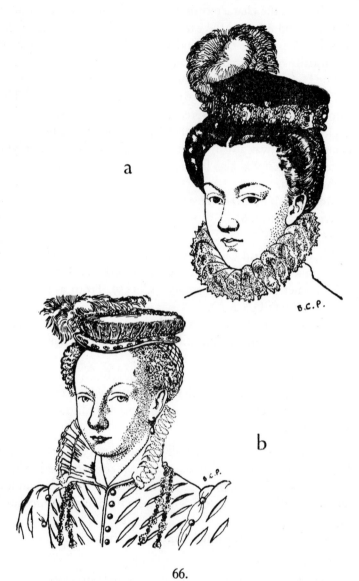

66.
(a) Court bonnet worn over a jewelled caul. (1575.) (b) 'Taffeta Pipkin' worn over hair net. (1575–80.)

B.C.P.

67.

Hat with tall crown, trimmed with jewelled hatband and large ostrich
feather; worn over an under-cap. Sleeveless gown with wings only.
Diaphanous covering to the kirtle sleeves and bodice. Gloves with
tabbed and trimmed cuffs. (1573.)

trimmed with a bunch of ostrich feathers upright or drooping.
A narrow jewelled hatband was usual. Worn over a caul or
hair net.

(b) *The Court Bonnet style* [1575–1585]. Worn over net or
caul.

(c) *The Small Brimless Beret* continued until *c.* 1560. It was
worn over an under-cap, and the hair was confined.

(d) *The Lettice Cap* [1500–1580's] continued, but was far
less in evidence.

(2) HATS. Hats with tall crowns and varying brims, trimmed with velvet, silk or cypress twists, or plain hat bands, were worn towards the end of the century, with or without under-caps or coifs.

'English burgher women usually wear high hats covered with velvet or silk for head gear.' 1599. Platters' *Travels in England*.

A low-crowned 'Bowler' was occasionally used.

Large plain straw Hats with coifs were worn by country women.

Materials as for the men.

'Two silke thrumed hatts . . . three felt hatts, and one taffitie hat.' 1582. Durham Wills.

Trimming. Hat bands as for the men.

Feathers as for the men. One or many might be worn.

'. . . an other sort . . . are content with no kind of hat without a great bunche of feathers of divers and sundrie colours, peakying on top of their heades.' 1583. Stubbes, *Anatomie of Abuses*.

In 1564 Queen Elizabeth wore a hat trimmed with 'a bush of feathers'. Nichols. *Progresses of Q. Elizabeth*, I, 160.

Embroidery mainly used for women's hats.

Pinking in patterns also employed.

OTHER HEAD WEAR

Reticulated Cauls. Some resembled hair nets, covering the back of the head, and might be worn alone, or under a bonnet. Some were shaped like French Hoods without the 'tail'.

They were made of goldsmith's work lined with silk, or of silk thread or of hair. 'Caps of haire that is not their owne.' 1605-1617. Fynes Moryson. *Intinerary*.

Trimming with lace, gold lace, ribbon, pearls and jewels was common.

'. . . Cawles made netwise to the end I think that the cloth of gold, els cloth of silver, or tinsell, . . . under their cawles, may the better appeare and shew itself in the bravest manner.' 1583. Stubbes, *Anatomie of Abuses*.

The nature of the lining might indicate the degree of social rank.

This applied also to partlets and sleeves (Sumptuary Proclamation, 1579.).

The Coif made in one piece with a seam along the top, was cut with a slight point over the forehead. The sides curved away from the temples, but forward round the ears and cheeks, to be tied under the chin. This was vulgarly known as 'cheeks and ears'.

'Cheeks and ears! . . . 'tis such as they wear a' their heads.' 1603. *London Prodigal* (Anon.).

Made of velvet or more often linen, which was richly embroidered with coloured silk and metal thread, black work or cut work.

Worn indoors, but not in bed, or

A plain style might be worn by invalids, or in bed.

'One Cambrick quaffe wroght with gold,

Quayffe wroght with red and blew,

Quayffes wroght with black,

Two night Quaffes (plain).' 1589. Inventory. E.R.O. D/D. Ba.

'three velvet night cappes'. 1582. Inventory. Durham Wills and Inventories.

The Forehead Cloth or Crosse-cloth [1580's–1700] was a triangular piece of material matching the coif with which it was worn. With the point behind, the straight edge was passed round the forehead and tied under the chin or behind the neck. Forehead Cloths were also worn with cauls and neckerchiefs.

'A cawle and three forehed cloths of cameryk netted with gold.' 1562. *New Year's Gifts to Queen Elizabeth* in Nichols'. *Progresses.* . . .

'My best two neckerchiefs with 3 cross cloathes.' 1577. Worthy. Devon Wills.

The use of Forehead Cloths is uncertain. They might have been worn to prevent wrinkles. They were definitely worn during illness. 'Many weare such crosse-clothes or forehead cloathes as our women use when they are sicke.' 1617. Fynes Moryson.

Voluper, a cap. 'Head-lace and veluper.' 1551. Middleton MSS.

The Arched Hood (1580's–1620, and rarely, to 1630). (Worn out of doors, and also connected with funerals and mourning.) Resembling a large calash, it was made of heavy material with one border threaded with wire, which was then curved so as to

a

b

68.

(a) Great arched hood worn over French hood and falling to the waist. Bodice with striped stomacher front; skirt with small French farthingale. (1599.) (b) Great arched hood trailing to the feet; worn over hair. Trunk sleeves puckered; kirtle rolled up. No farthingale. (1586.)

make a great arch over the head. This arch was often bent so as to project forward into a point above the forehead. The side supports were fixed to the shoulders, or less often to the waist, the wearer appearing to be standing in a porch. The drapery might be gathered in at the nape of the neck or waist, or allowed to flow freely down the back to varying lengths. It was worn alone, or over another headdress.

N.B. A bare head, or merely head ornaments or cauls, were considered quite correct, even out of doors, and was fairly common from the 1560's, especially with 'young married women and virgins.'

'The women are beautiful, fair, well-dressed and modest, which is seen there (in England) more than elsewhere. . . . Married women only wear a hat both in the street and in the house; those unmarried go without a hat, although ladies of distinction have lately learnt to cover their faces with silkin masks or vizards. . . .' 1575. Van Meteren, *Nederlandtche Historie.*

HAIR

Throughout this period the *back hair* was plaited or coiled behind the head, and generally hidden by the headdress or decoration. *The front hair* varied, but always left the forehead uncovered.

Front Hair Styles

(*a*) From a centre parting the hair was waved, or less often, arranged in close curls, and in both cases bunched out at the temples [1540–1575].

(*b*) From a centre parting the hair was turned back over a pad with fulness at the temples [1560–1570's].

(*c*) The parting was eliminated, the hair being raised over a wired support or 'Palisadoe', generally given a dip in the centre, but still widening at the temples.

'which of force must be curled, frisled and crisped, laid out on wreathes and borders, from one ear to another, and lest it should fall down, it is underpropped with forks and wires and I cannot tell what. . . .' 1583. Stubbes, *Anatomie of Abuses.*

The same effect with a broader curve was produced by pads

over which the hair was often arranged in close curls [1570's–1600].

A *freak fashion*, arising from the above, with the hair wired up into two upright horns, was foreign and of short duration [*c.* 1595–1600].

After 1590 the central dip was omitted.

False Hair, Wigs, and Dyed Hair were all in use.

Hair Ornaments.

The Billiment was in great favour, and was frequently double, an upper billiment worn high round the built-up coiffure, and a nether billiment worn forward and lower. Some were made of bands of silk, velvet or satin, lined and garnished with jewels. Others were made of goldsmith's work, gold billiments being suitable for brides.

The prices varied much

'An upper billimente lyned with satten 4s.

An nether billimente of black velvet 3s.

An nether billimente of white satten 2s. 4d.

For 2 billimentes of golde, an upper and an nether, enamyled white £16 16s. for the fasshion of the said billimentes.' 1559. Petre Archives. E.R.O. D/DP. A9D.

Fillets, or narrow ribbon bands 'wherewith women doe wreath and bind their haire', ribbon bows and separate jewels were frequent after 1580.

'Fyllettes, Two harelaces.' 1589. E.R.O. D/D. Ba.

Patches (1595 to the end of the eighteenth century). These were made of velvet or silk cut into small pieces of varying shape and applied to the face by means of mastic. A patch might hide a blemish or 'act as a foil to beauty'.

> or Gellia wore a velvet mastick patch
> Upon her temples
>
> 1598. Hall's *Satire I.* Book VI.

Powder and Paint were also used.

LEG WEAR

STOCKINGS (sometimes called Nether Stocks, or even hose), were tailored, or knitted, the latter becoming increasingly common. Stockings reached above or below the knee, and might have clocks.

Materials. Wool for the poor, silk for the rich. But a fairly wide range of materials was used according to the type of stocking required.

> *Sumtyme they will beir up thair gown*
> *To schew thair wylecote* (petticoat) *hingeand* (hanging) *down*
> *And sumtyme bayth* (both) *they will upbeir,*
> *To scew* (show) *thair hois* (hose) *of black and brown.*
> 1556. *Satire on the Town Ladyes* by Sir Richard Maitland.

> *Thy crimson stockings, all of silk*
> *With gold all wrought above the knee.*
> 1584. From *A New Courtly Sonnet of the Lady Greensleeves.*

Two pairs of stockings might be worn together, as with men. '... hir nether stockinges worsted, coulour watchett (blue), clocked with silver, and edged on the topps with silver, and next hir leg, a payre of jarsye hose, white, ...'. 1587. Narrative of the Execution of Mary Queen of the Scots in a letter to Sir William Cecil.

SOCKS were also worn by women.

'Payed ... for half a dozen of sockes for my Ladie.' 1576. Petre Archives. E.R.O. D/DP. A9G.

GARTERS. Were embroidered bands or sashes, tied below the knee.

'A payre of green silke garters' (1587) were worn with the two pairs of stockings quoted above.

> *Thy garters fringed with the gold*
> *And silver aglets hanging by.*
> 1584. *The Lady Greensleeves.*

SHOES AND OVERSHOES were similar to those worn by men. 'Because your pantables be higher with cork, therefore your feet must needs be higher in the insteps.' 1591. T. Lyly, *Endimion.*

PUMPS were popular. 'Thy pumps, as white as was the milk.' 1584. *The Lady Greensleeves.*

STARTUPS were worn by countrywomen.

> And in high startups walk'd the pastur'd plaines,
> To tend her tasked herd. . . .

1597–1598. Hall's *Satire I*, Book VI.

BUSKINS worn for riding.

ACCESSORIES

GLOVES. These resembled those worn by men, scented or 'sweet gloves' being very fashionable. 'A payre of newe sweet gloves' were exchanged for a pig in 1592. (Essex County Session Rolls.)

'A peire of gloves p'fumed and cuffed with golde and silver. A peire of gloves, with lowpes of golde lyned with crymson vellat. Two peire of working gloves, silke knit.' 1556. Nichols, *New Year's Gifts to Queen Mary* in *Manners & Expences* . . . .

MITTENS with one compartment for the fingers, the thumb being separate, were worn towards the end of the century. They were as elaborately embroidered as the gloves, not only on the gauntlet by occasionally on the back of the hand.

APRONS OR 'NAPRONS'

(*a*) Aprons often with bibs and brightly coloured were worn by the working classes and country housewives.

(*b*) Aprons without bibs were worn by ladies in the home and also as *elegant accessories*, especially towards the end of the sixteenth century, a fashion lasting until 1640 and revived in the eighteenth century.

Materials

(*a*) Holland, canvas, dowlas, linsey-woolsey, worsted, flannel, durance.

(*b*) Cambric, linen, silk, taffeta. Trimmed with cut-work and edged with lace.

HANDKERCHIEFS OR HANDKERCHERS. Similar to those carried by men and usually as large; made of lawn and trimmed with lace; or embroidered and sometimes fringed and tasselled.

'Six handkercheives of white work (cut-work); five handker-

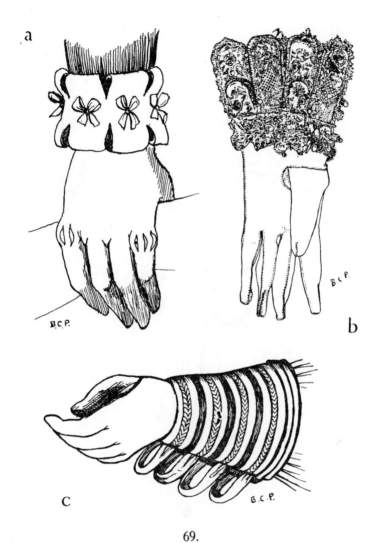

69.

Gloves for men or women. (a) Glove of style before 1585. (b) Glove of
style after 1585. (c) Glove of style verging on 1600.

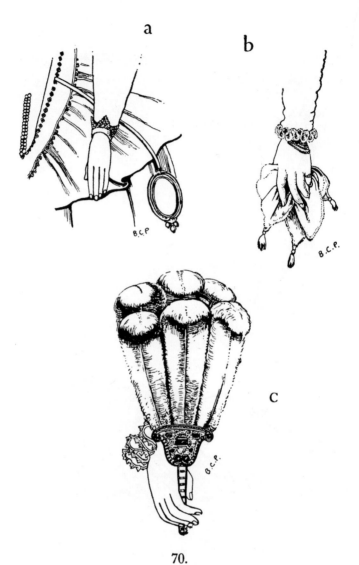

a

b

c

70.
(a) Small oval mirror hanging from the waist. (*c.* 1599.) (b) Tasselled handkerchief. (1571.) (c) Ostrich fan with jewelled handle. (*c.* 1575.)

cheves wrought with golde and red silke. Six handkercheves frenged and tasselled with gold.' 1556. Nichols, *New Year's Gifts to Q. Mary*, Ibid.

Handkerchiefs of the poorer classes were of coarser materials such as holland, and for utility only.

'16 Karchers of hulland 20/. 10 Kerchers of callecow 5/.' (Inventory of Joan Redwoods, widow. City of Exeter Records.)

NECKERCHIEFS *or* KERCHIEFS were worn round the neck or over the head. 'Six frowes (crimped) kercheves playne.' 1556. Nichols Ibid. 'Hollan cloth [for] hir nyghtkerchers'. 1552. Middleton MSS.

THE GIRDLE was of ribbon, silk or goldsmith's work, usually having one long pendant portion in front ending with an attached pomander or jewel.

A DEMICENT also was worn.

ARTICLES SUSPENDED FROM THE GIRDLE by ribbon or chain; A purse, a Fur Stole, a Muff, a Fan, a Mirror, a Pomander, or 'a boke covered in velvett to hang at her girdell'. 1550. Ibid.

The Purse was a small bag drawn in by strings and often of rich materials trimmed with gold or silver. 'A purse of blewe silke and golde.' 'A purse of red silke and gold knyt.' 1556. *New Year's Gifts to Queen Mary* in Nichols. *Manners & Expences . . .*

Other Materials used: Velvet, tynsel, satin, cloth of gold or silver, also russet.

The Fur Stole of marten or sable, lined with silk, satin or velvet, plain or the head and claws mounted in gold inlaid with jewels, continued to be worn, either round the shoulders or slung from the girdle (See Section I).

The Fan was usually made of feathers, radiating from a decorative handle often of silver. A small mirror was sometimes let into the base. Others were made of silk or straw. 'Seven fannes, to keep of the heate of the fyer, of strawe thon (the one) of white silke.' 1556. Nichols, *New Year's Gifts to Queen Mary*. Ibid.

The folding Fan began to be used in the 1580's.

The Mirror resembled that described under Men, and was usually small and round or oval. 'A looking glasse of christall

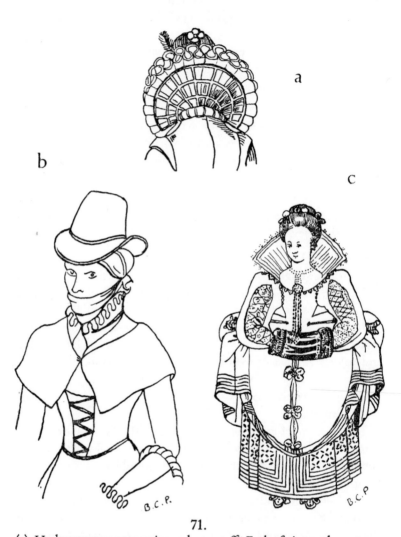

71.

(a) Underpropper supporting a large ruff. End of sixteenth century.
(b) Countrywoman with chin-clout. (1574.) (c) Rebato round the
back of the neck; skirt hitched up showing decorated underskirt.
Carrying small muff. (End of sixteenth century.)

coverid with crymson vellat, embraudered with golde and silver.'
1556. *New Year's Gifts to Queen Mary*, Ibid.

The Muff (also called Snufskin, Snowskin and Skimskyn while
small, 1580 onwards).

At the end of the century women's muffs were small and tubular; and when not in use were often slung from the girdle. They
were made of fur or silk, with trimming or embroidery. 'One
snoskyn of crymson satten.' 1599–1600. Nichols, *Progresses of
Queen Elizabeth*.

Scarves made of silk, cypress, lawn, taffeta, often fringed or
tasselled with gold or silver, were worn round the neck for
warmth, or show.

'Then came her Grace (Queen Elizabeth) on horsebake (apparelled) in purpull welvett, with a skarpe about the neke.' 1558.
Machyn's diary.

THE MUFFLER (sometimes called chin-clout). [1535–1660's.]
This was a large square of material diagonally folded and worn
over the chin and mouth, and occasionally included the nose. It
appears to have been used at times for disguise. 'We will all be
muffled for knowing (i.e. that we should not be known)'. 1566.
Caveat for Common Cursitors. Thomas Harman, 'Now is she bare-
faced to be seen, straight on her muffler goes.' 1594. *The Cobler's
Prophesie*. 'I spy a great peard under her muffler.' *c.* 1600. *Merry
Wives of Windsor*, IV, ii. (Falstaff dressed as a woman.)

Materials used. Black satin, taffeta, velvet, with sarcenet for a
lining.

'A mufler of purple vellat, embrawdred with Venice and
damaske golde and perle.' 1579. *New Year's Gifts to Queen
Elizabeth* in Nichols. *Progresses of Q. Elizabeth*.

THE MASK [1550's–1760's], covering the whole face, or the half
mask covering the upper part, was used in public to avoid
recognition, or out of doors as a protection for the complexion.
It was oval in shape, with holes for the eyes.

Made of velvet, silk, satin, taffeta, and lined with thin skin or
silk. The button attachment on the under surface whereby the
mask could be held in place by the teeth, was occasionally present.

Colours varied.

> But on each wight now are they (masks) *seene,*
> the tallow-pale, the browning-bay,
> The swarthy-blacke, the grassie greene,
> the pudding red, the dapple graie.

1595. S. Gosson. *Pleasant Quippes for Upstart Gentlewomen.*

JEWELLERY. Long chains of goldsmith's work used as necklaces, and often partly caught up with a brooch. These might also be used as girdles. Lockets, pendants, bracelets, pomanders, rings and earrings, and jewelled buttons. Gems of all sorts (sometimes sham) were lavishly sewn on to garments worn at State functions. A dress was said to be 'flourished with pearls' when these were peppered over it. Fantastic jewelled ornaments, corresponding with the insect and animal embroidery motifs, might also be worn.

Hans Jakob von Breuning, who was presented to Queen Elizabeth, wrote the following description of her apparel in 1595: '. . . dressed in some silver garment adorned with a wonderful array of magnificent jewels . . . . Her Majesty's bosom was bare and framed in a pair of open-work or transparent ruffs (the fan-shaped ruff) upon the front of which she had placed a horrible huge black spider looking absolutely natural and alive'.

PINS were used in large quantities.

'Item pd . . . for a thowsen of clowt pinnes 8d.' 1555. Petre Accounts E.R.O. D/DP. A9A.

Pins were a toilet necessity for 'the trymmynge and pynnynge up of theyr gere . . . prycke them and pynne them as much as ye wyll, and yet wyll they loke for pynnynge styll'. 1547. J. Heywood, *The Four PP.*

CARCANET

(*a*) Gold collar, often jewelled. 'Bye for me as many of the fairest pearls . . . to make a carcanet.' 1605. St Clare Byrne (ed.), *Elizabethan Home.*

(*b*) A similar ornament for the head. 'Curled haires hung full of sparkling carcanets'. John Marston. *Antonio and Mellida.* 1601.

Working People's Clothes

In style, the dress of working people differed sharply from that of upper classes, being not only much plainer but presenting out-moded fashions. It varied, but not in adaptation to particular forms of work so much as for economic reasons. Suffice it here to consider manual workers, especially those of the country, crafts-men and tradesmen, especially in towns, seamen and the servants of large households.

MATERIALS

'Husbandmen weare garments of course cloth made at home . . . and their wives . . . gowns of the same, . . . kirtles of some light stuffe with linnen aprons. Their linnen is course and made at home.' 1605–1617. Fynes Moryson's *Itinerary*.

For the poorest, the chief materials were coarse woollens known as kendall (generally green), russet (generally brown), frieze or simply 'cloth'; and mixtures of wool and yarn such as linsey-woolsey. Fustian was in general use, 'serving mean people for their outsides and their betters for the linings of their garments'. (1662. Fuller's *Worthies*.) Shirts, underwear and linings were of coarse linen such as lockeram for the better off and canvas or sackcloth for the poorer.

> He had a shyrt of canvas hard and tough
> This was a husbandman, a simple hinde.
>   *c.* 1568. *Debate between Pride and Lowliness.*

Hose were cut from blankett or 'cloth'; knitted materials were somewhat of a luxury for most of the period.

Silks were used only by the wealthier tradesmen and household servants. In the poem quoted above, 'cloth breeches' stood for the poor man and 'velvet breeches' for the rich. Various skins and cheap furs were much used.

72.

(a) Queen Elizabeth's grooms wearing royal badge on the jerkins of their livery. (1575.) (b) Gardener in long, sleeveless jerkin, long loose breeches. (1594.) (c) Ordinary groom in tunic-like coat, tied in front. 'Tights' with cod-piece. (1563.) (d) Workman's sandal-like shoe. (1563.)

MEN

Manual workers

For manual workers three characteristics of 16th-century fashions obviously had to be eschewed—the unwieldy puffed shoulders of Henry VIII's reign, and the distended trunks and large ruffs of Elizabeth's. The garment most often in evidence was knee or thigh length, loose and belted—in fact like a mediaeval tunic. This would possibly be the doublet itself or else an overgarment, that is a 'cote' or, even at the beginning of the century, a 'jerkin' (Jerkins for the upper classes came in the latter half.)

Other jerkins were sleeveless and often made of 'skynnes'. The cote seems to have been less common with labourers than with servants and townsmen. (See below.) Doublets were plain and jerkins sometimes fastened at the side.

Gowns were seldom worn, stomachers, partlets and close-fitting jackets never. For hard work the doublet was removed and the shirt sleeves rolled up. Already there was a characteristic 'wagoner's frock' (1585. Junius' *Nomenclator*), which was probably a loose garment like the later 'wagoner's smock-frock'.

Leg wear all through the century might consist of long joined hose like 'tights', in fact of typical 15th-century style, sometimes soled and worn without shoes (Fig. 36b, p. 95), sometimes even footless. From at least 1530 onwards, loose baggy breeches or 'sloppes' with separate 'stockins' or stockings were an alternative for any country wear. This was long before wide sloppes became the fashion. Narrower breeches like those of Fig. 55a, covering the knee but left untidily open below, were used towards the end of the century. See Fig. 72b.[1]

A Ploughman wore thick tab-fastened boots and with them over-stockings.[2] 'Startups' were an alternative, i.e. the ankle boots which were characteristic of working men for the next three centuries, becoming known in the 18th and 19th centuries as 'highlows'. The wooden pegs mentioned in the quotation on p. 129 were a means of fastening sole to insole and still used in recent times for wader

[1] Woodcut in *The Orchard and the Garden* (1594).
[2] Engraving in J. Fitzherbert's *Boke of Husbandrye* (1525).

73.
Merchant in cloak, short cassock, breeches, ornamental garters, copotain hat. (1598.)

boots. The wood swells when wet and does not rot too easily. Other country shoes were often described as 'double soled'.

For extra warmth a hooded cape was still worn. Cloaks were indulged in only by the better off: a well-to-do grazier wore

> *A jerkin made of buffe*
> *A fair cloake upon his backe*
> *And on his head a felt* [hat or cap].   Ibid.

Summer hats were of straw.

Tradesmen, Craftsmen

The townsman's clothes smacked more of fashion than the countryman's but often followed the styles of one or two generations earlier. The humblest still wore 'tights' but others went in for paned trunk hose in the '60's, German style. See Fig. 36a. The strips from the panes or the tufts tended to hang loosely about their thighs. Short-sleeved or sleeveless jerkins and short gowns were not unusual. Footwear included simple shoes, like sandals, and mules. Very characteristic was the head-gear, as described on p. 133.

The garb of an elderly man of the poorer class at the end of the century was probably not unlike that of the miser described below, still wearing the styles of Henry VIII's reign in 1596. 'Band wears he none, but a welt of course Holland . . . His truss is the piece of an old pack cloth . . . His points are the edging of some cast pack saddle. . . .

His jacket forsooth is faced with moth eaten budge, . . . and in his bosom he bears his handkerchief made of the reversion of his old tablecloth. His spectacles hang beating over his codpiece like a flag in the top of a maypole. His breeches and stockings are of one piece. . . . His shoes of the old cut, broad at the toes . . .' Thomas Lodge, *Wits Miserie*, 1596.

A merchant, near the end of the century, would wear a loose hip-length cassock (cf. Fig. 55a), breeches gartered below the knee, a short cloak and a copotain hat.

For certain groups there were distinctive features of dress. Apprentices wore blue. Butchers and cooks wore washable aprons

74.
Sailor in short cassock, slops, and thrummed cap. (1598.)

194

of coarse linen such as dowlas. Smiths, tanners, cobblers and carpenters used large bibbed aprons of leather.

> '*What trade art thou?*' '*Why, sir, a carpenter.*'
> '*Where is thy leather apron and thy rule?*'
> 1601. Shakespeare *Julius Caesar*, I. i. 58.

Already barbers were distinguished as 'checkered apron' men.

Bakers wore functional white caps. A stranger 'handsomely apparelled' but wearing a 'white knitte cappe' was recognised for a townsman and 'judged a baker by trade' in *c*. 1568. *Debate between Pride and Lowliness.*

The ceremonial livery of the city companies consisted of a long gown of more or less contemporary style, and a mediaeval hood which was now an anachronism. It had developed a curious bucket shape and its 'liripipe' (now 'tippet') could be used as a handle.

Seamen

The wearing of sloppes by sailors, afterwards such a characteristic of their dress, began in the 16th century. These might be 'long strayte sloppes' such as were designed for the 'Palmers' in a masque at court in 1554;[1] but more typically they were extremely baggy breeches closed below the knee. (The 'Palmers' and 'Mariners' alone wore sloppes instead of hose at this masque—the pilgrims, no doubt to show up their poverty in an otherwise glamorous company.) For typical seamen ashore a hip-length straight cassock put on over the head, shoes and stockings and a thrummed hat or cap completed the outfit.

Household Servants

Men employed in large households dressed comparatively well. They were a privileged class whose clothes were provided and the best of them inherited some of their master's cast-offs. Those in the menial ranks were clad more or less like country folk in good circumstances. A 'boye of the kichyn' in 1520 had a 'doblett and coate' made for him. 'Canvas for to make him a shirt . . . blanckett to make a payer of hose', shoes and 'clowte

[1] . . . *Office of the Revels at the time of . . . Q. Mary*, ed. A. Feuillerat.

lether' to mend them with, were all supplied. (Lestrange Accounts.) Again 'Lytell John of the Kichyn . . . a cape for him' is recorded in the Middleton MSS, 1527. In 1575 there was a 'jerkin, dublet and breeches' for the kitchen boy. (Ibid.)

The middle-ranking servants—the main body—wore livery, which became very dashing in the 16th century. Though the trunk hose were frequently white, the upper garment was so often blue (probably indigo, 'butcher blue') that 'blue-coat' became synonymous with 'servant' in contrast to 'russet coat', the yokel. The Shifter in Chettle's *Kind-Harts Dreame* (1592) put his two accessories into blue coats so as to appear to be a gentleman accompanied by servants. In a satire on the Serving Man's profession written in 1598, we read of 'the yeoman or Husbandman's sonne, aspyring from the Plough to the Parlor' and how 'his ambitious desire of dignitie . . . moved him to change his habite and cullour from Jerkin to Coate, and from Russett to Blew." ('I.M.' *A Health unto the Gentlemanly Profession of Serving Man.*' ed. A.V. Judges, 1931.)

A popular alternative colour to blue, for liveries, was tawny.[1] 'xj peces of brodcloth made at Rideng the colour light taweny orange colour for leverys for my master's servantes.' 1522. Household Accounts of Sir Thomas Lovell in Middleton MSS.

Sometimes the family's armorial colours were displayed in a parti-coloured livery. The horse attendant's coat in Fig. 8b (p. 34) was in fact half one colour and half another. Whatever the colour of the material, the family's badge was generally blazoned upon it, for example an 8-inch Tudor Rose on the doublets of Queen Elizabeth's attendants. If not embroidered it could evidently be appliquéd:

'Crimsyn satten for Roses for iiij Riding Cotes for ij yomen of the gard'. 1517. Henry VIII's Wardrobe Book.

In the later years the badge was often worn as an engraved or embossed metal plate fixed to the sleeve.

The seasons were allowed for. The Willoughbys of Notting-

---

[1] It is not always clear whether colour or material are meant when terms like tawny and marble are used. 'viii Brodeclothes of tawne' were dyed at Wollaton with madder, a natural red dye. 1525. Middleton MSS.

hamshire and the Petres of Ingatestone Hall, Essex, both had livery of 'marble' in summer and frieze in winter. (That of the Willoughbys was trimmed with 'blew lace'. Middleton MSS. pp. 403, 448.)

In royal and noble households a great variety of people were issued with elegant liveries. Henry VIII's 'five groomes of our preavie Chamber' and 'oure two barbours' had 'cootes of grene clothe styched with grene silke—having buttons of like silke— lyned with frise and fustian.' 1535/6. (*Archaeologia*, *9*, 248). Queen Elizabeth's master cook had a 'coate of marble cloth garded with vellat'. (B.M. MS. Egerton 2806, f. 25.)

In 1597 a Sumptuary Law against the use of silks by working men ends with this exception:

... 'but her Maties servantes and the servantes of noblemen and gentlemen may weare such lyverye coates or clokes as their masters shall give or allowe unto them, with their badges and cognizances or other ornamentes of velvet or silke, to be layed or added to [them]'. (Egerton MSS. p. 255).

Fynes Moryson, in *Itinerary* (1605–1617) writes. 'The servants of gentlemen were wont to weare blew coates with their Masters badge of silver on the left sleeve, but now they most commonly weare clokes garded with lace, all the servants of one family wearing the same liverie for colour and ornament. ...'

A servant would still go armed when his master 'walked abrode'. He would 'take his livery and weapon', to set out, 'being himself ready, handsome and appoynted.' 1598. 'I.M.' *A Health unto the Gentlemanly Profession of Serving Man.*

WOMEN

The typical working woman, dressed for action, wore a kirtle with front fastening bodice, short sleeves and a skirt that was ankle-length, for the young, and foot length for the older woman. The hem of this she turned up and fastened to a waist girdle, revealing an under petticoat. Farthingales were not used. A rail or neckerchief went over the shoulders and a long apron hung from the waist. For work no overgarment (gown), would be worn, no ruff, and the headdress would be a simple veil or kerchief or even

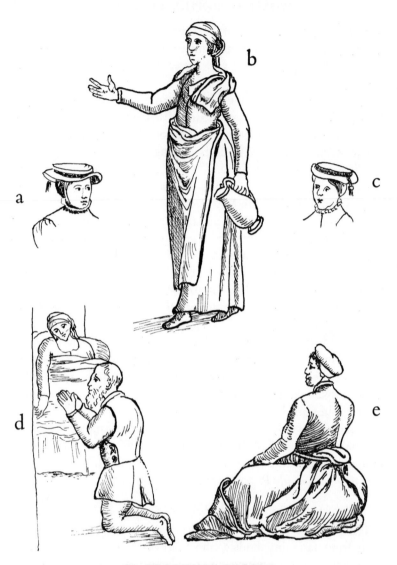

75. WORKING PEOPLE

(a) and (c) Townswomen's hats with flat-cap style crowns. (b) Working girl, straight kirtle, long apron, neckerchief and kerchief round head. (d) Her sick mother wearing a cross-cloth and night-smock, her father in sleeveless jerkin tied at the side. (e) Woman with skirt tucked up under belt. (All 1563.)

ribbon fastened over the head. A model country girl is described
by Thomas Churchyard as she cleans the house in 1575.

> *And at her gyrdle in a band*
> *A jolly bunch of keyes she wore*
> *Her petticoat fine laest before*
> *Her taile tucke up in trymmest gies*
> *A napkin hanging o' er her eies*
> *To kepe of [f] dust and drosse of walles*
> *That often from the windows falles.*
> > *The Spider and the Gowte* in *Churchyardes Chippes.*

Out marketing, and therefore smarter, a woman is seen in a
miniature part of which is shown in Fig. 71b. She wears a plain
buff gown and beneath it a red kirtle. The latter shows under the
lacing of the bodice; also through the open front of the gown
skirt, except where both are hidden by a large white apron. She
wears tiny ruffs at neck and wrists, a white coif, a grey felt hat
and a white tippet over the shoulders. The chin-clout is of course
an occasional accessory.

Alternative headwear was, for townswomen, in flat-cap style,
like the men's, worn over an undercap (1560's). When the
'statute cap' (p. 133) was ordered for men:

'in the tenth or twelfe yeare of Queene Elizabeth . . . and for
three or foure yeares after, all Citizens wives . . . were constrayned
to weare white knit Caps of wollen yarne, unlesse their husbands
. . . could prove themselves gentlemen . . . and then ceased the
women's wearing of *minevor* Caps [i.e.] three-corner Caps. These
minevor caps were white, and three-square, and the peakes thereof
were fully three or foure inches from their head'. Howes' additions
to Stow's *Annales* (edn. 1631) p. 1039.

Accessories for townsfolk included chin-clouts and gloves.
The woman in Fig. 71b had a fowl in one hand and a basket in the
other, but nevertheless carried gloves. However her whole attire
is untrimmed and very plain compared with that of even a merchant's wife, to say nothing of the gorgeous array of her upper
class contemporaries.

Women domestic servants did not normally wear livery, but

were comparatively well dressed, especially in rich households. The complete outfit supplied to 'a mayde' in Queen Elizabeth's Court was as follows:

'A black fryse cassocke with poyntinge rebande and two fustian pockettes and lyned collar and ventes: sixe lynen Aprons: one Apron of fuste mockeado: foure cutt koyves [coifs]; foure cutt kercheves, foure other kercheves: two peire of hpse: a wastecoate of red kersey: a felte hatt: foure peires of Showes: foure cawles and foure Smockes: two petycoates, one red cloth th' other stammel fryseado, upperbodied with mockeado, lyned with fustian, frenged with cruell, lyned about the skyrtes wth bayes.' 1575. B.M. MS. Egerton 2806, f. 92.

Children's Clothes

At birth all children were wrapped in swaddling bands over a shirt and sometimes a biggin (cap) or simply over a cloth. Older babies wore long clothes with a bibbed apron and a muckinder hanging from the waist girdle.

Boys were dressed as girls up to the age of 5 or more. They were then dressed like their fathers, though rather more often in loose slops.

Girls wore ground length skirts and in their teens were dressed almost exactly like their mothers. Fig. 56 shows Princess Elizabeth aged 13 or 14. In the upper classes girls even suffered the discomfort of (moderate) farthingales and ruffs when these came in. There was one difference: they did not have elaborate headdresses. At most they might wear billiments or simple coifs on special occasions.

Clothing materials for children were generally cheaper than for adults, russett being commonly used, even in upper class families.

The following is a contemporary account of clothing supplied by their guardian to the orphan son and daughter of Sir Henry Willoughby (Willoughby Accounts in Middleton MSS.).[1] The boy is stated, in another Middleton MS., to have been 2 years old in 1548 and his sister to have been older. She must still have been quite a little girl when the accounts open in summer 1550, since she was supplied with 'counters to learn to caste withal'. We will assume, on all the internal evidence, that the boy was now just 3 and the girl about 11.

The Girl, Margaret
   Aged c. 11. (1500) 'black russell for a *kyrtell.*[2] . . . *bone lace* for her

[1] Household Account of Sir Thomas Lovell in Middleton MSS. (Hist. MSS. Commission, 1911).
[2] All italics ours.

76.

Baby and two girls wearing aprons, the little girls in grown-up style,
except for farthingales and ruffs. One wears a coif. Boy unbreached, in
double-skirted doublet over a long skirt. He carries a plumed hat and
wears a sword. (1596.)

necke . . . blacke ryband for *gyrdells* . . . a thousand *pynnez* . . . a hundred *nedells* . . . red brode clothe for a *petycote* . . . halfe a yearde of redde russell for *upper bodyez* for the same . . . buckeram for a *varthingale* and for redd clothe for the same, for laying buckeram in [her] *gowne*. . . . *Shoez* . . . an ivery *combe* . . . *frose paast* (headdress, see p. 77) . . . carseye to make . . . *hossen* a boke covered with velvett to *hange at hir girdell*.'

Aged *c. 12* (1551) '*Clooke* garded with velvett . . . payre of satten *slevez* . . . *headelace* and *veluper*' (cap).

Aged *c. 13* (1552) 'hollan cloth to make *nyght-rayelles* and *nyght kerchers* . . . a payer of *bresselettes* 60 elles of lynnen for *frosekerchers* (headdress) *slevez* and *pertlettes*.'

Aged *c. 14* (1553) (Keeping her own accounts). 'Cloth for *ruffez* for my brother and me. . . . a *calle* for me.'

Aged *c. 15* (1554) (Still a growing girl:) 'Satten . . . *to lett downe* her crymsen damaske *kyrtell* . . . a *bongrace* . . . *whoode, bylamentes* and *muffelers*.'

Ages *c. 16* (1555) (Presented at Court) 'An *upper abylament*, a *nether abylament* and a *crypen* (of a French hood) a cloth *gorgett*.'

The boy, Francis

Aged *5* (1550). 'A payre of *Knytte hosen*[1] twoe yerdes of whyght fustyan to make *sloppes*[2] . . . bockeram for a fustyan *doublett* . . . a *gowne* . . . (of russet, with fustian for the "bodyes" and cotton for the pleats) . . . for *claspez* . . . a grenne *coate* . . . dossen of *poyntes* . . . a taffyta *coate* an ell of fustyan to make *slevez*. . . .'

Aged *6* (1551). 'A velvett *nightcappe* . . . whyght carseye for *upper stockez*.'

Aged *7* (1552). 'A taffita *hatt* . . . twyle to line *hosen* . . . *shyrtes* (linen) . . . A skynne and a halfe to make . . . a *jerkyn*, for russetting of the same . . . Spanyssh skynne for a jerkin.'

Aged *8* (1553). 'A sechell for . . . *bokez* . . . black fryse to make a *coate and hosen to ryde in* . . . *ruffez* . . . For pollyng him.' (Haircut).

---

[1] A boy in his early teens was wearing 'knitt hose' even in 1530 (Lestrange Accounts), and as it seems unlikely that children would be given imported fashions this may mean that knitting was established in England earlier than is generally supposed.

[2] The slops were probably loose undistended breeches.

Aged 11 (1556). (Now at boarding school) 'A *felte hatte for workadyez* . . . sackcloth to make him a *gowne* . . . two fox skynez and dim ($\frac{1}{2}$) to fase the same. . . . '

Aged 13 (going 'to schole wyth Docketer Carre' at Cambridge) . . . 'twoe yeardes rattes color cloth to make him a *gowne* . . . a *knytt cappe* . . . furre to lyne him a *gowne* . . . furred *glovez*.'

The completeness of a mere schoolboy's wardrobe in *c.* 1570 is revealed in the following:—

The lad was a late riser and is shouting to the maid:

'Geeve me my hosen . . . my doublet . . . my garters and my shooes . . . Geeve me that shooying horne.' Margaret suggests a 'clene shirte.' Then 'Where have you layde may girdle and my inckhorne? Where is my gyrkin (jerkin) of Spanish leather, of Bouffe?, Where be my sockes of linnen, of wollen, of clothe? . . . my cap, my hat, my coate, my cloake, my kaipe, my gowne, my gloves, my mittayns, my pumpes, my moyles (mules), my slippers, my handkerchief, my poyntes . . . where is all my geare?' Claudius Hollyband. *Dialogue 1.* ed. M. St. Clare Byrne in *The Elizabethan Home*, 1949.

Less is known about the children of the poor, but a note given in John Stow's *Annals* (1592), may be worth quoting.

'On Christmas Day (1552) when the Lord Maior . . . rode to Paules, all the children of Christ's Hospital [founded that year] stood in array . . . all in one liverie of russet cotton, the men children with red caps, the women children kerchiefes on their heads.'

Appendices

For evidence, the Henry VIII Wardrobe books and Inventories, (one published in part and three unpublished) have been extensively drawn upon. The sources of quotations from these are indicated simply by their dates. Reference to the list of Sources (pp. 228–234) will complete the citations.

APPENDIX I. HOSE

A few notes will be made on three topics.

A. *Upper and lower portions—joined or separate?*

When the breech and the lower-leg covering differ in material, while there is no visible free end to the latter nor garter to support it, the question remains whether the two were actually joined together—and if so how. Take first, styles before trunk hose.

The term 'hose' could certainly be used for the entire covering from foot to waist. In the Wardrobe documents of Henry VIII dating 1516/17, 1520/21, 1535/36 and 1547 respectively, this was the rule. The entire 'hose' is treated as one garment whether differentiated into upper and lower stock or not, and the hose were generally part of a suit—often 'doublet hosen and jacquet' (1516/17).

'. . . doblet and hoses of purpull velvete and black tylsent paned and cutt after th' alamayn facon [German fashion]'. (Ibid.)

'One jerkin of purple vellat with satten sleves of purple colour . . . and a paire of hoose of purple satten and like embroderie.' (A gift, 1545.)

In the Inventory of 1520/21 there is no independent list of legwear, upper or lower. Thirty-two descriptions of doublets end up with the words 'with hose to the same'. By that date some at least of the hose must have had differentiated upper and nether stocks. It is hard to believe they were not united to make the one 'pair of hose,' at least by temporary stitching.

The 'one garment' view is supported by the very many warrants in 1535/36 of which this one is typical:

'A paire of grene clothe hoose, upperstocked with grene velvette, fringed with gold, lyned'; and rather revealing is a warrant for alterations:

'For translating a paire of upperstockis of purple velvett . . . tuffed with cameryke . . . as also for making a newe pair of nether stockis to the same.' (Ibid.) The upper portions were always more ornamental than the lower and also did not wear out as fast. These same circumstances may account for the absence of netherstocks to the specimen of padded ring (trunk) hose now preserved in the London Museum.

The only exceptions to the treatment of the legwear as a single garment are these. (a) There is a solitary example where two pairs of netherstocks were made for one pair of upper (quoted on p. 35). (b) A single odd pair of 'netherstockes' appears in the published extract of the 1535/36 list—otherwise there are no clear references to stockings (in our sense), as separate articles. (c) Four pairs of 'stockis', one 'of taffata', three 'of Geneva clothe' are mentioned (Ibid). As these were embroidered and lined with skarlette they may have been residual upperstocks.

In the later Inventory made in 1547, though there is a long list of 'Hoose', again there is no distinction into upper and lower garments. Most of the hose are of satin, embroidered etc., but a number are 'silk and gold knitt', and one is of 'gold and silver knite like unto a caule'. Possibly the knit ones were indeed separate nether stocks (so often called, later, 'knit hose'). There is also a single example of an odd upperstock. This, described in detail, was a gift to the King in 1542, with the doublet that it matched. Presumably, had ready-made whole hose been presented, they would not have fitted. One wonders whether the suit was ever completed and worn.

As regards trunk-hose proper, if without canions, the consensus of opinion seems to be that the upper and lower parts were indeed joined together and it would be difficult to imagine how, when there was no garter, the stockings would present their usual smooth appearance unless dependent on the breech. Either stitching, or continuous lining could have been used. Cloth hose had always been lined throughout. 'To the Kendall man for xx yerds of hose lynyng for the children'. (Lestrange Accounts, 1553.) Even the 'slops' type of breeches had a lining 'straight to the leg' as well as the distending linings. It therefore seems possible that in trunk hose there was sometimes a continuous lining from waist to ankle. Where the nether stock was knitted presumably it would depend on stitching, not lining.

Howes, in his additions to Stowe's Annales (Edn. 1631), wrote of the London apprentices and journeymen, 'at the time of Queen Mary and the beginning of the Reigne of Queen Elizabeth and for many years before . . . their Breeches and Stockings were usually of white broadcloth, viz. round Slops, and their stockings sowed up close thereunto, as if they were all but one piece.'

B. Some special types of legwear.

The Inventory of Henry VIII's wardrobe, 1547, includes 'Trunkes to shoote in' (the only 'trunks' mentioned) and 'Arminge hoose of crimson yellow sattin embrawdrid wt scallop shells . . .'

Lord North had 'a doublet and hose, of leather' in 1578. (Household Book of Lord North.)

Warrants of Henry VIII, 1516/17, read: '. . . Grene velvete for stocking of ii payr of lether hose for the King' and 'A yerde $\frac{1}{4}$ crimosyn saten for a payr of stalking hose.'

Andrew Boorde recommended men to 'Use lynnen sockes or lynnen hosen next your legges'. (Dyetary of Helth, 1542.) It was probably underwear of this kind that is meant by 'thirtie paire of hose and thirtie paire of sockis of fyne lynnen clothe' for the King, in 1535/6.

In all the four Wardrobe documents of Henry VIII only two 'pairs of sloppes' are recorded. At this time loose sloppes were probably too informal for His Majesty.

A unique entry which suggests an advance towards Venetians in 1516/17 (ambiguous though it is), reads: $2\frac{3}{4}$ yards 'of blake tylsent damaske gold for the upper partes of a payr of hose to the knee, all of tylsent [i.e. not paned?] garded with the same.' (Ibid). More than twice as much material was needed here as for the usual upperstocks.

How bizarre was the fashion in legwear, at the end of the century is shown by the following, written in early Stuart times:

'Memorand that over the seates in the parlment house at the parlm't Anno 43 Eliz. was certaine Holes 2 inches square in the walls in which was placed posts to uphold a scaffold round about the house for them to sitt on which vsed the wearing of great breeches stuffed with haire like woolsackes which Fashion being lost . . . the Scaffolds were then pulled down. . . . (Hare 980 p. 235.)

C. Meaning of the terms 'Stocks' (unqualified) and 'to stock'.

The term seems to have applied both to the upper and to the nether stocks. Only the context shows what is meant.

'To Hilton [tailor] iii yerds of grene tylsent for a doblet. To William hosyer . . . a yerde [and a] quarter of grene tylsent for stockes for hoses to the same'. (1516/17.)
Here upperstock is meant. Countless orders specify, and contemporary pictures confirm, that it was this part of the hose (if either) that would be made of the same material as the doublet. Again:—

'one yard [and a] quarter cloth of silver for the stockes of a payr of hose. 1 yarde quarter cloth of damaske gold to cover the said stockes.' (1516/17.) Such a quantity and arrangement could only apply to upper-stocks. Again: 'Crimosyn velvete to be cutt upon a pair of stockes of crimosyn tylsent.' (Ibid.)

The frequent and easily misunderstood expression 'the stocking of' or 'to stock' a pair of hose generally meant to complete them with an *upper-stock*. A warrant for a green velvet doublet is followed by one 'for grene velvet for stocking of a payr of hose to [match] the same.' (1516/17.) Again:
'iii quarters of cloth of silver damaske silver to be panyd with blake tilsent for stocking a of payr of hoses.' (1516/17.) Only upper-stocks could be paned.

Unfortunately in Elizabeth's time 'stocks' often meant netherstocks, either as part of trunk hose or as separate stockings worn with breeches. The attire of the Earl of Leicester, celebrating a feast of the Order of St. Michael in 1571, was thus described:

'. . . His stocks of hose knit silk; his upper-stocks of white velvet (slashed and) lined with cloth of silver.' (Nichols in Trans. Leics. Archaeol. Soc. II, 323.)

Again, two men in the Queen's household in 1575 were supplied with identical pairs of gascons but one received at the same time 'nether stockes of stammal kersey' while the other had 'knitt stockes'. (B.M. MS. Egerton 2806, 91.)

Stomachers, Placards, Partlets.

All of them denoting fronts or fill-ins, nevertheless these are not synonymous terms. Thus, all three occur side by side, and frequently, in the royal wardrobe lists of 1516/17 and 1547. The King's placards and stomachers each took $\frac{1}{2}$ yard of material or less, to make, while his partlets took $1\frac{1}{2}$ yards or more.

Men's Stomachers. In the 1516/17 Wardrobe book at least thirteen 'stomagers' in different coloured satins occur, and others in 1535/6. These last are usually lined but not embroidered. Stomachers were perhaps designed merely to make a neat background to the lacing or front ties of a doublet.

Men's Placards. Most of these were certainly made for doublets, usually to match the sleeves or foresleeves.

'Doblett of russett cloth of gold ⎫ the placards and fore-
Doblett of crimosyn satten ⎬ sleeves of every of them
Doblett of damaske sylver ⎭ richly embroidered'. (1516/17.)

'doublet of blacke satten with placard and foresleves of blake tinsell crested with black velvet.' (Ibid.)

Less exalted personages also had placards and foresleeves to match. (See pp. 19 & 21.)

'Placards' of some kind were made to match the base and horse's trappings used in riding. The King had several sets, e.g.

'A Base wt. a placard of white cloth of gold tissewe to wear upon horses wt. a rich trapper to the same.' (1516/17.)

Men's Partlets. As these generally took 1½ yards of material, and even 'iii yerdes of grene velvette for a long partlett' (1516/17), possibly they had a back as well as a front panel.

They were made specially to go with jackets: 'x yerdes russet saten for a jacket and a parlet.' Some 'lytell partelets' occur in the 1520/21 Inventory and these are listed with the 'Somer Jacquettes'.

Partlets were essentially ornamental.

'One partlet of crimson vellat wt.owte sleves all over embroderid with venice golde and silver stiched wt. purple silke lined wt. crimson satten.' (1547.) As explained on p. 61, sleeves were never an actual component of an partlet.

Women's Stomachers were already worn in 1516/17. '½ yard of playne tylsent' and the same amount in a dozen different coloured satins made thirteen 'stomagers' for the Queen in 1516/17. In 1547 was listed 'a stomacher of white satten embroidered about with flatte golde and damaske pirles lined with white sarsenet' among women's clothing.

The Elizabethan stomacher is fully described on pp. 155, 156.

Women's Placards in the 1547 Inventory are listed as 'placards for gowns', 3 of tissue, 1 of cloth of gold, 8 of velvet and 14 of satin. They appear to have been neither embroidered nor lined, perhaps merely being a background to lacing.

Women's Partlets could be very ornate like the men's, but much smaller, covering only the upper breast and/or neck. (See p. 61.) Usually ½ yard of material was needed, sometimes less:

'halfe a yarde and di. [½] quarter of . . . velvet for partlettes.' (Household Expenses of Princess Elizabeth, 1551.)

A 13-year-old girl's partlets were simply 'of lynnen'. (1552, Willoughby Accounts); but they could be made of anything from jewelled gauze (Queen Elizabeth's portrait at Penshurst Place) or 'Lawne wrought with gold about the collar' (1547) to 'purple velvett embraudered with perles of damaske golde garnished with small perles and precious stones, lined with white satten.' Ibid. The latter had an exactly matching muff.

'Twooe Partlettes for women, *tall fashion*, of Venice gold' occur in the 1547 Inventory.

Partlets were often made to match either detachable sleeves or wrist ruffs. In 1562 one of Queen Elizabeth's New Year presents was 'a peire of sleves and a partelett'; and in 1556 Queen Mary received three sets of 'a partlet and a peire of ruffes', one 'wrought in gold and blewe silke.'

Glossary of Materials

[E.E.T.S. = Early English Text Society]
[E.R.O. = Essex Record Office]

'I note a nother grete mysordur in the apparayle, I say, of our people. For now you se ther ys almost no man content to were cloth here made at home in our country, nother lynyn nor wolen, but every man wyl were such as ys made beyond the see, as chamlet, says, fustyanys, and sylkys. . . .' *England in the Reign of King Henry, VIII* Pt. II *A Dialogue* . . . by T. Starkey (temp. Henry VIII). E.E.T.S. Extra Series, 32, p. 94.

BATH CLOTH. A fine quality of woollen textile.

BAUDEKIN. A rich silk woven with gold and having a raised pattern. Coloured purple, white, green, blue, crimson, vermilion and murrey. 'Branched cloth of Bodkin.'

BAYS. A napped woollen fabric, lighter than modern baize. 'Five yards of bays worth 12/5.' 1581. (Essex County Session Rolls.)

BENJAMIN. 'The aromatic gumme called benjamin or benzoin.' (Cotgrave) used in perfume for gloves, etc.

BLACKS. Black cloaks, hoods etc. supplied at the cost of the deceased to certain mourners.
'Blackes sowld for the funerall of Mrs. Lenard.' 1584. (Lenard Accounts.)
'item 17 yards fyne black at 14/.' (E.R.O. D/DL. F47/2.)

BLANKET CLOTH. A white woollen cloth.

BLUE. (*a*) A colour.
(*b*) A material, nature uncertain. 'A gown of brown blue £3.' 1587. (City of Exeter Records.)

'One ell of cloth called brode blewe worth 12s.' 1566. Assize File 35/8/1 (Essex).

'Blue 11/½ to 1/3 a yard. Striped 10¾yd. Prented 11d. a yd.'. (1691–1694. Woolhope Club. Trans.)

BOMBAZINE. A material of silk and wool or silk and cotton. At first dyed black but later in various colours.

BORATTO. 'A light stuff of silk and fine wool.' (Sewell.)

BRANCHED OR BRANCHT. Figured.

BROADCLOTH. See CLOTH.

BROCADE. 'A fabric with a pattern of raised figures.' (Beck *Drapers' Dictionary*.)

BUCKRAM. A coarse linen (or cotton) textile. Cf. LOCKRAM. '1 pr of buckram hose . . . 12 yards of buckram for my daughter's gown.' 1522 and 1533. (Lestrange Accounts.)
Also used for lining and stiffening; variously coloured; red, yellow, etc.

BUCKRAM CANVAS. Buckram stiffened with gum, starch or paste.

BUFFIN. A type of grogram.
'The buffin gown with the tuft-taffety cap.' (*Eastward Hoe* J. Marston *et. al.* 1605.)

BUREL. A coarse woollen cloth.

BUSTIAN. A coarse fustian.

CADDIS. A woven tape used for garters, girdles, etc. Sometimes a woollen weave, coarse or fine.

CAFFA. A rich silk, variously coloured, used by Tudor royalty.

CALICO OR CALICOWE. A cotton or cotton and linen fabric imported from the East and costly. Coloured red, blue, green or yellow.

CALIMANCO. A material of wool or silk woven in irregular patterns.

CAMBRIC. A fine linen fabric, so fine that the 'greatest thread' was 'not so big as the least hair that is.' (P. Stubbes. 1583.) Varied in quality, priced from 2/- to £1 an ell (45 inches.)

CAMLET OR CHAMLET. Probably a kind of mohair or, later,

camel hair cloth, mixed with wool, silk and cotton, and having a watered appearance. 'My silk chamlet kyrtell.' (Wayman Wills. 1535.) 'For 1½ yardes of redd grogramne chamblet for the upper bodies of two petticoats at 4/4 the yarde.' 1559. (E.R.O. D/DP. A9D.)

CANVAS. A hempen cloth made in several qualities; very popular for doublets. 'Tufted canvas' was a coarse linen. 'For 3 yardes of striped canvas for a dublett at 2/4 the yarde; for coarse canvas to lyne it.' 1569. (E.R.O. D/DP. A9F.)
(A plain weave woollen canvas is modern.)

CARRELLS OR CURRELLES. A mixed fabric of silk and worsted or sometimes linen yarn. 'Three yards of orange tawney carroll worth 5/.' 1589. (Essex County Sessions Rolls.)

CENDAL. Similar to and largely replaced by sarcenet from the fifteenth century onwards. 'My petticoat of sendall.' *Greensleeves.*

CLOTH. A woollen textile with a long history and many laws aiming at ensuring its purity and cleanliness, e.g. in 1597 when flocks, sollace, flour, chalk and 'other deceitful things' injurious to cloths were employed making them 'rewey, squally, cockling, light and notably faulty'.
BROADCLOTH was a fine woollen cloth of plain weave, 2 yards wide.

CLOTH OF GOLD. A cloth woven with gold wire or with flat strips of the metal or both. The gold threads were generally woven with silk, but occasionally only gold was used.

COBWEB LAWN. A very fine linen textile.

COLOURS. *Ash-grey.* 'A hose lynying for his asshe colerd hose.' 1530. Lestrange Accounts.
Beauty. A colour the shade not known but often mentioned during the first half of sixteenth century. 'A gowne of bewticolour lyned with blak.' 1508–1509. York Wills.
Brassel, Brazil. A red colour obtained from the brownish-red wood of an East Indian tree.
Bristol red. 'London hath scarlet and Bristowe pleasant red.' c. 1513. (Barclay's Fourth Eclogue.)

Cane colour. Yellowish tint.

Carnation. Resembling raw flesh. Blount. *Glossographia,* 1656.

Clodie-colour. 1600. Nichols. *Progresses . . . of Q. Elizabeth.*

Crane colour. 'A doublet of crane coloured satin.' 1556. (E.R.O. TA 482.)

Gingerline. Reddish violet. (Corruption of French Zinzolin.)

Goose-turd. Yellowish green.

Gosling colour. 1600. Nichols. *Progresses of Q. Elizabeth.*

Hair, heare. Bright tan.

Horse-flesh colour. Bronze.

Incarnate. Red.

Isabelle or Isabella. Greyish yellow or light buff.

Lady-blush. 'loose gowne of ladie-blush satten' 1600. Ibid.

Lincoln green. A favourite colour for archers.
'Lincoln anciently dyed the best green in England.' (Selden.)

Lustie-gallant. Light red.

Maidenhair or hair. Bright tan.

Marble. Parti-coloured resembling marble. 'My gown of marbell colour.' 'A payre of hosses (hose) of marble colour.' 1519. (E.R.O. D/DL. F.153.)

Medley. A mixture of colours.

Milk-and-water. Bluish-white.
'A blew cote, one milk and water jerkin.' 1589 (Leeds Wills.)

Murrey. Purplish-red, but having a considerable variation.

Orange. A very popular colour in the sixteenth century.

Orange Tawney. An orange brown.

Peach. Deep pink.

Pear or Catherine pear. Russet red.

Plunket or Blunket. Light blue or sky blue.

Popinjay. Green, or blue, or a mixture, 'a yerde of Popynjaye grene satten of brydys'. 1520. (Lestrange Accounts.) 'Popinjay blue.' 1577. (Harrison's *Description of England.*)

Primrose. Pale yellow.

Puke. A dirty brown. The camel's colour. '1½ yard puke kersey.' 1569. (*The Great Orphan Book.*)

Rat's colour. A dull grey; used for funeral gowns of poor men.

Roy or Couler de Roy. A bright tawny.

Sad. Any dark shade. 'A cloke of a sad newe culler.' 1570. (City of Exeter Records.)

Sangyn. Blood red.

Scarlet. A vivid red containing yellow.

Sea-green. Bluish or yellowish green. 'For a yarde and a half of frizardo sea water greene to make my Master a jerkyn.' 1589. (E.R.O. Petre Accounts.)

Sheep's colour. Neutral. 'My new cloak of sheeps colour.' 1561. (E.R.O. T/A. 48/1.)

Stammel. Red.

> *The bonny damsel fill'd us drink*
> *That seem'd so stately in her Stammel red.*
>
> 1594. (Greene, *Friar Bacon and Friar Bungay*.)

Straw. A light yellow.

Tawny. A brown tinged with orange or yellow.

> *For black and tawnie will I wear*
> *Which mourning colours be.*

(Earl of Oxford's *Complaint of a Lover*, temp. Elizabeth.)

Watchet. A pale greenish blue. 'For a payer of boothose, watchet colour.' (E.R.O. Petre Accounts.)

Whey. A pale whitish blue.

Willow. A light green.

Yellow. A very popular colour in the sixteenth century.

COVENTRY BLUE. Thread of a vivid blue, chiefly used for embroidery.

CRAPE. A thin transparent textile of silk or silk and linen, made to have a crimped surface.

'A crumpled silk stuff.' Generally dyed black and used for mourning, see Cyprus.

CREWEL. A two-threaded worsted commonly used for garters, girdles and small wear, also for trimming.

'A coote and a cappe of green cloth fringed with red crule.' 1535. (Dress of Henry VIII's fool.) *Archaeologia* 9.

CRISP. Crespin or Creppin. Similar to crape and often used for women's head coverings.

CYPRUS, CYPRESS OR SIPERS. A thin transparent textile of silk or silk and linen, similar to crape but it might be smooth or crimped ('curled.') 'Smooth sypars at /7 the yd. Currelled sypars at 1/ the yd.' 1586. (City of Exeter Inventory, No. 3.)

DAMASK. A rich silk fabric with an elaborate design woven into the texture. True damasks were of silk, but the term came to be applied to any fabric of wool, linen, or cotton woven in the same way. 'a kertell of damask, the bodys of saten old, lined with yello cotton 10s.' 1524–1525. (Inventory of John Port. Nichols' *Manners and Expences 15th, 16th, 17th Centuries.*)

DIAPER. Usually a linen textile patterned by opposite reflections from its surface and used for household purposes.

DIMITY. A fine fustian with linen thread, woven in diagonal stripes.

DOWLAS. A coarse linen fabric largely used by the poorer classes for shirts, aprons etc. Bakers used it for sieves. Compare buckram and lockram.

'I bought you a dozen of shirts to your back.'

(Falstaff) 'Dowlas, filthy dowlas. I have given them away to bakers' wives and they have made boulters of them.' (*Henry IV*, Pt. 1, III. iii. 79. Shakespeare, 1598.)

DRUGGETT. A wool fabric or wool and silk or sometimes linen.

'For 17 yards of gold drugget to make me a sute and coat.' 1655. (Expense book of James Masters *Archaeol. Cantiana*, 15–18.)

DURANCE. A closely woven worsted fabric, being strong and enduring. Cf. Perpetuana.

'An apperne (apron) of durance /12.' 1590. (City of Exeter Records.)

'6½ yds. of crimson durance at 2/8 the yd.' 1594. (Shrewsbury tradesman's invoice.)

'Durance of Duretty with Thread, and Durence of Duretty with Silk, are mentioned in Charles I's Charter of 1640.' (Beck.)

ESTRICH, ESTRIDGE wool or felt. Ostrich down, used for hats as substitute for beaver.

'17 estridge feelts untrymmed at the rate of 10/ the dozen.' 1586. (Inventory of Exeter Hatter.)

FELTED KNITTING. A process whereby a knitted article, usually a cap, purposely knitted about three times too large, was soaked in water, rubbed and pummelled by heavy stones to produce felting and shrinkage to the correct size. (See article 'Wool Knowledge' by James Norbury. 1952.)

A number of these caps have survived, see Victoria and Albert Museum and Christchurch Mansion, Ipswich.

FERRET. A stout cotton tape or silk ribbon.

FLANNEL. A fine soft cloth of open texture, made of woollen yarn slightly twisted in the spinning. Very common for warm waistcoats.

FRIEZE. A woollen cloth with a heavy nap on one side, typically for working dress; but

'A coarse kind of cloth ... than which none warmer to be worn in the winter, and the finest sort thereof very fashionable . . . the gentry being much impoverished,' (Fuller's *Worthies*. 1662.)
Variously coloured; also black or white.

FRIZADO. Similar to but of better quality than frieze. '1 ell tawny Frysado 4/.' 1565–1566. (Essex County Sessions Rolls.)

FURS. *Armins*, i.e. ermins.

Badger.

Bear.

Beaver, also called Castor. Used for hats. Three qualities:
1. New castor. The winter coat, a rich fur.
2. Dry castor. Summer coat and of thin poor quality.
3. Fat castor. The old coat and greasy.

Budge, Bugg, Bogy. Lambskin with the hair dressed outwards.

Calaber. Grey fur of a small animal the size of a squirrel. (Originally from Calabria.)

Castor. See Beaver.

Cat. 'An old gowne faced with catts skynne. 6/8.' 1560 (City of Exeter Records.)

Cony (rabbit) very popular. 'A gowne of rattes color furred with white lambe and faced with conye. 20/.' 1571. (City of Exeter Records.) 'Greye coneys (and) grissel connies' Petre Records for 1589. (E.R.O.)

Cordwain or Cordovan leather. Best Spanish leather.

Elk. 'A cloke of elkes skinnes'. 1547. (Henry VIII's Wardrobe.)

Ermine. for the nobility.

Fitch or Fitchcock. Polecat fur.

Fox. 'A gowne of Kentis blewe faced with fox.' 1560. (City of Exeter Records, bundle 1–52.)

Foyns. Marten.

Fuchals. Polecat, see Fitch. 'A gowne furred with fuchals.' 1571. (City of Exeter Records.)

Genet (or Jennet). A kind of civet-cat.

Grays or Gris. Marten.

Hare. 'For XI whyte hares at XVI d. apece for furring of 2 gownes of sacke cloth.' 1556. (E.R.O. D/DC. A9C.)
    'Outlandish hare' was a foreign import.

Lamb.

Lettis or Letewis. A fur resembling ermine. Cotgrave states that Letice was a beast of a whitish grey colour.

Leopard. 'Mantilles of lyberdes woombes [belly]'. 1517. (Harl. 2284.)

Leuzernes or Luzerne. Lynx.

Marten.

Miniver or Meniver. 'The fur of ermines mixed or spotted with fur of the weasel called gris.' (Cotgrave.)

Mink.

Moale. Mole.

Neat's leather. Hides of the bovine species.

Otter.

Pampilion a fur. 'a gown . . . for the Quene of Scottes . . . for two Skynnes of pampelyon for the cuffes of the . . . gown.' 1503. (Expenses of Elizabeth of York.) Also a felt.

Rabbit. 'For two dozen of blacke rabbettes skyns at two pence the pece.' 1569. (E.R.O. D/DP. A9F.)

Racoon.

Sable.

Shammoy. Chamois. 'For 4 shammoys skyns at 5/ the pece (to make) a payre of shammoye hosen.' 1570. (Petre Archives.)

Shanks. A common fur obtained from the leg of a kid or sheep. 'My newe furre of shanks.' 1518. (Will of Margery Wymond, daughter of a London grocer.)

Squirrel. 'Gown of scarlet faced with foynes and furred with squirrels.' 1579. (City of Exeter Records, 28a.)

Stote.

Wolf.

FUSTIAN. A fabric of cotton and flax, or flax mixed with wool, and having a silky finish. Used as a substitute for velvet. Very popular for all garments.

FUSTIAN ANAPES. (à Naples). 'Mock velvet or fustian anapes.' (Cotgrave.) Until the seventeenth century fustians were imported and often named after the source of supply e.g. Jean (Genoa) fustians, Milan fustians.

'2 yardes of holmes fustian to make . . . a dublett 20d.' 1555. (E.R.O. D/DP. A9A.)

GAUZE. A woven silk fabric of transparent texture; also sometimes made of cotton or linen.

GROGRAM. A material of mohair, silk, or worsted in taffeta weave, and having a coarse grained texture. 'Their gowns be no less famous than the rest, for some are of silk, some of grogram, some of taffetie, some of scarlet (a material) and some of fine cloth.' 1583. (P. Stubbes, *Anatomie of Abuses.*)

HARDEN. 'A common linen made from tow, or the coarsest quality of hemp or flax.' (Beck, *Drapers' Dictionary.*) Often used for sheets, but also for lining servants' garments. 'V yards of gray ... iii yards d. of harden lyning for him ... ' 1618. (Howard Archives, Naworth Castle.)

HOLLAND. A fine linen of various qualities.

HOUSEWIFE'S CLOTH. Described as 'a middle sort of linen cloth between fine and coarse for family uses' (*Chambers's Encyclopaedia* 1741); but was also a kind of russet e.g. 'Two pieces of cloth called huseyfes russett containing four yards worth 5/.' 1559. (Chelmsford Assize File. 35/1/7. 18.)

INKLE OR INCLES. A linen tape varying in width and quality; used for girdles, garters, apron strings, and cheaper sort of trimming. Usually yellow but might be red or blue, or striped red and blue or pink and blue. Inkle sometimes meant the thread from which the tape was made.

JEAN. A twilled cotton textile.

JEANES FUSTIAN. May have contained wool. See Fustian.

JERSEY. Very fine wool.

KENDALL. A coarse woollen or cotton fabric coloured green.

> *All the woods are full of outlaws, that in Kendall green,*
> *Follow'd the outlaw'd Earl of Huntington.*

> 1597/8. A. Munday. *Downfall of Robert, Earl of Huntington.*

KERSEY. A double-twilled say, coarse or fine, and variously coloured. e.g. 'skye culler, russet, greene, gilliflower, sad new culler, white.' 1578. (Inventory of a clothier of Kirbye.)

LACE. Billiment lace was gold or silver.

Parchment lace, called guipure in France, was another kind of gold and silver lace.

LAWN. A very fine and costly linen widely used for ruffs, collars, cuffs, kerchiefs and rails in sixteenth and seventeenth centuries.

LINEN. A material woven from flax.

LINSEY-WOOLSEY. A loosely woven cloth made of linen yarn and wool.

'A waistcoat of linsey-woolsey.' 1589. (Essex County Sessions Rolls.)

LIST. The selvedge.

LOCKRAM. A coarse loosely woven linen with relatively finer varieties (see Buckram). Used for shirts, neck wear, coifs, etc. of the poorer classes. 'lockeram for the making of cotes for the boyes in Heywoodes play'. 1553. Feuillerat, . . . *Revels . . . in the time of Q. Mary.*

LUKES. Materials classified with velvets. Velvet of Luke. (Lucca.)

MARBLE. A parti-coloured worsted interwoven so as to resemble the veining of marble.

MEDLEY. A cloth woven with different coloured wools. (See Colours.)

MILK AND WATER. A material the nature of which is uncertain. (See Colours.)

MOCKADO. Sometimes called Mock Velvet. A piled cloth of silk and wool, or silk and linen. Colours varied; it might be plain or striped and tufted, the pile being of a different colour from the ground. 'For making a frize jerkin . . . for a yarde of fustian for the boddyes . . . for half a yarde of mockado to face yt.' 1580. (E.R.O. D/DP. A10.)

MOTLEY. A worsted of mixed colours giving a mottled effect.
  '1 mottley clooke bagge 2/.' 1604. (City of Exeter Records. 85.)

MUSTERDEVILLIERS. With many variations of spelling. Its nature uncertain. Frequently mentioned in fifteenth, sixteenth and seventeenth centuries. Fairholt describes it as 'a mixed grey woollen cloth'; Stow as a mustard-coloured material. It has been suggested that the name is a corruption of 'moitié velours'; or derived from a French town called Muster de Villiers.

MYLLION. Milan fustian, the latter word often omitted.
  'A piece of millyan fustian worth 10/.' 1588–1589. (Essex County Session Rolls.)
  'White myllion.' 1597. (City of Exeter Records.)
  'For 3 yardes 1 quarter half of white myllion.' 1576. (E.R.O. D/DP. A9G.)

NETTLE CLOTH. 'This may have been made of the fibres of nettles. . . . appears in an inventory of 1572, priced at 1s. the yard'. (Beck. *Draper's Dictionary*.)

OLDHAM. A coarse woollen cloth.

OSNABURG. A coarse linen or fustian.

PENNISTONE, PENNYSTONE. A fine frieze of variable quality, usually white and then known as FOREST WHITES, but also coloured.
  'Bought at Bartilmew Fayer 4 peces of penystons whites, contayning eche of them II yarde and more after 22/9 the pece.' 1555. (E.R.O. D/DD. A9A.)

PERPETUANA. A strong lasting material resembling serge; in

many colours, often black. 'The sober Perpetuana suited Puritane.' 1606. (Dekker, *The Seven Deadly Sins of London*.)

'6 yards d. of green perpetuana at 3s. 4d.' 1618. (Howard Archives, Naworth Castle.)

PLEASAUNCE. Described by Strutt as 'a fine species of gauze, striped with gold'. Used for head-coverings.

PLOMMETTS. Probably similar to CARRELLS.

PLUNKET. 'A sort of coarse woollen cloth' (Bailey). But a richer quality was also made. '7 yardes of plunket cloth worth 40/.' 1649. (Essex County Session Rolls.)

'... came six ladies all in crimosin plunket embroidered with golde and perle.' (Reign of Henry VIII.) (See also Colours.)

PLUSH. A silk fabric having a longer nap than velvet.

POLDAVIS. A coarse linen.

PUKE. A woollen textile dyed before weaving. Of varying quality. '1 yeard ¾ of blak pewk 7/. i yeard and ½ of blak pewk £1.' (In 'the lytele shop' of John Wilkinson of Newcastle.) (See Colours.)

PURLE. Thread or cord made of twisted gold or silver wire, and used for embroidery or decorative borders.

RASH. A twilled textile of silk or wool, of varying quality but generally not a rich material. 'Payed in London for 3½ yardes of tawney Raishe for my ladyes gown at ii/ the yarde.' 1576. (E.R.O. D/DP. A9A.)

'A dublet of Rasshe 5/.' 1577. (City of Exeter Records.)

RAYNES. A cloth of a fine quality of linen.

RUG. A warm shaggy frieze, largely used as a lining or for winter, especially by the poor. 'For half a yarde of rug to stiffen ye dublett 17 d.' 1581. (E.R.O. D/DP. A10.)

'Like a subsister (a poor begging prisoner) in a gowne of rug rent on the left shoulder'. 1592. (Chettle's *Kind Hearts Dream*.)

RUSSELLS. A worsted with a lustrous surface like satin. Coloured black, white or red. A sixteenth-century material revived in the eighteenth century.

RUSSET. A coarse woollen homespun sometimes known as SHEEP'S RUSSET. Usually in natural colour or reddish brown, but also black and sometimes other colours. Largely used by country folk.

> Courtier, whose hart with pride so mighty grows
> Thou wilt not to thy Father moove thy Hat
> Because he weares a paire of russet Hose
> Thy velvet Breeches looke awry at that.

> 1604. (S. Rowland's *Look to it: For Ile Stabbe ye.*)

'5 yardes of blake russettes at 3/6 the yard.' 1555. (E.R.O. D/D. PA9G.)

Cotton Russet is mentioned in the Privy Purse Expenses of Elizabeth of York 1502/3.

Silk Russet is mentioned in Essex County Sessions Rolls in 1581 as worth 9/ a yard. (See Colours.)

SACKCLOTH. In the sixteenth century this was far less coarse than sacking of earlier or later times, and was used for outer garments. It varied in quality, colour and design; it might be fine or coarse, marbled or striped. 'Fifteen yards of straw-coloured sackinge redd stryped, worth 12/.' 1589. (Essex County Sessions Rolls.) (See also quotation under FUR, Hare.)

SAMITE. 'A silken or half-silken stuff, which hath a gloss like satin, and is narrower but lasteth better than it.' 1611. (Cotgrave.) Sometimes interwoven with threads of gold and silver and often embroidered. Coloured red, white or black.

SAMMERON. A fine linen used for sheets, see HARDEN.

SARCENET. A fine soft silk of taffeta weave. Largely used for linings. Variously coloured, green, white, tawny or 'changeable' (shot).

SATIN. A glossy silk fabric with a smooth surface. Variously coloured, e.g. crimson, green, purple, sky, tawny, yellow, popinjay, black or white. Branched satins (i.e. figured) also occurred. 'Satin of Bridges' is Bruges satin.

SAY. A fine twilled fabric of wool or silk and wool in the sixteenth century, though subsequently all wool and resembling serge. Varying in width. 'Elbroade sayes, yard brode sayes.' 1597. (Shop inventory City of Exeter Records.)

'Double sayes or Flander serges.' *c.* 1638. (Book of Rates.)

'Sayes called silk sayes.' 1592. (Lansdowne MS.)

Red, green blue, watchet or black.

SCARLET. A very fine worsted cloth. 'A yarde and quarter of scarlet at 17s the yarde.' 1555. (E.R.O. D/DP. A9A.)

SERGE OR SIRGE. A twilled worsted stuff.

SHAG. A thick piled shaggy cloth of worsted or silk, sometimes of goats' or camel's hair. Generally used for linings. Coloured scarlet, blue, buff or black. 'My silk grograine coate lyned with red shagge which I wear when very sick.' 1644. (Will of the Countess Rivers.)

SILK. 'The written records of the Chinese empire are said to carry back a knowledge of the treatment of silk to a date 2700 B.C.' (Beck, *Drapers' Dictionary*.) Imported to England in the twelfth century and on; first manufactured in London by foreigners *c.* 1662.

SINDON. Linen or silk, possibly both.

SIPERS. See Cyprus.

SLESIA LAWN. A fine linen resembling cambric.

STAMIN, ESTAMINE OR TAMIN. A fine silk and wool fabric.

STAMMEL. A fine woollen cloth possibly a variety of kersey.

'Kersies in the shop: carnacion K. English stammel, coarse sky coloured K. Vassey sky K. Osett red K.' 1569. (City of Exeter Record, 13.)

See Colours.

STRAITS. A narrow cloth, e.g. 'yard wide straits'.

TABBY. A watered silk. 'To tabby, to give a wavy appearance to stuffs with the calender, to water.' (Wedgwood.) (Whence 'tabby cat'.) Sometimes striped.

TABINET OR TABINA. Like poplin. A thick silk or silk and wool, calendered to give a moiré surface.

TAFFETA OR TAFITY. 'A light thin silk stuff with considerable lustre or gloss.' (Beck.) Very popular in the sixteenth century. Made in many colours, also shot ('changeable').

Imitation Taffeta in linen was used at the end of the sixteenth century 'viii yards lennen taffety 12/.' 1582. (Inventory of a Newcastle merchant.)

Tuft-taffeta or Tufted taffeta was woven with raised spots or stripes cut to produce a velvet pile which was of a different colour from the ground; thus producing a very decorative material. Much in demand by the rich, even for their head wear. 'sleeveless his jerkin was, and it had been velvet; but was now (so much ground was seen) become tufftaffaty.' (Donne, *Fourth Satire*.)

TAMINE. See STAMIN.

TAUNTON. A broadcloth made at Taunton.

TAVISTOCK. A broadcloth made at Tavistock.

TAWNY. A woollen cloth usually yellowish brown in colour.

THRUMS. The threads at 'the extremity of a wever's warp often about nine inches long, which cannot be woven'. (Richardson.) Thrummed material was made of wool or silk, with a long nap to produce a shaggy surface and used for hats. Woollen thrummed hats were largely displaced by Spanish felts for the aristocracy in the second half of the sixteenth century.

TIFFANY. A thin gauze-like material of silk or silk and linen. Largely used for linings puffed out through slashes, or for head rails. 'A drawne worke coyfe, a silken tiffany to weare over it.' 1615. (Essex County Sessions Rolls.)

TINSEL, TYLSENT OR TILSON. A rich sparkling fabric of silk interwoven with gold or silver thread. It might be coloured crimson, green or black. 'Pair of sleeves of crimson tynsell . . . ditto of green tynsell.' 1523. (Inventory of Dame Agnes Hungerford.)

TISSUE. A variety of cloth of gold, made of precious metals and silk in twisted threads, variously coloured purple, russet, green, white; largely used by royalty. 'Eight yerde of sea greene tyssue for double slevis for two ridinge gownes.'

1612–1613. (Warrant to the Great Wardrobe on Princess Elizabeth's marriage.)

TUKES. A kind of Buckram.

TULY OR TEWLY. 'The name of a silk or thread made in the sixteenth century.' (Beck.) 'For half an ell of twilley to line them' i.e. frieze breeches. 1580 (E.R.O. D/DP. A10).

VELVET. A very popular material among the upper classes in the sixteenth century. Velvet (as also Taffeta) was sometimes stiffened with gum 'but the consequence was that the stuff thus hardened quickly rubbed and fretted itself out.' (Beck.)

'I have removed Falstaff's horse and he frets like a gumm'd velvet.' 1598. (*Henry IV*, II ii.)

VERDOURS, VERDURES. Not identified. ? green baize.

VESSES. A sort of Worsted.

WADMOL. A coarse woollen textile; largely a poor man's material for doublets, jerkins, etc. Dyed blue, murrey, etc.

WHALEBONE. 6 yards of whalebone cost 1/- in 1612.

WOOL. 'That wool is eminently the foundation of the English riches, I have not heard it denied by any.' (Sir Joshua Child, writer on Trade in 1630–1699.)

'The first actual mention of the sheep occurs in a document of the year 712, when the price of the animal is stated to have been fixed at 1/- until a fortnight after Easter.' (Beck, *Drapers' Dictionary*.)

WORCESTERS. A fine quality of woollen cloth.

WORSTED. A woollen textile made from well twisted yarn, smooth and strong.

Sources

A. PRIMARY

Manuscripts

British Museum MSS.

Egerton 2806. Warrants to the Great Wardrobe (1568–1588).

Harl. 2284, 'Wardrobe Book of Henry VIII.' (The King's Warrants in 1616/17.)

Harl. 4217. Inventory of Henry VIII's Wardrobe at the Tower, in 1520/21.

Harl. 1419 A. & B. Inventory of Henry VIII's Wardrobe remaining at his death. (1547; additions 1551.)

Harl. 6064 (containing rules for ceremonial and mourning attire, temp. Queen Mary and Queen Elizabeth).

Essex Record Office, Chelmsford. Many MSS. especially the domestic accounts of the Petre family, and Wills.

Essex Assizes Files.

Essex County Session Rolls.

Exeter, City of, Records.

Public Record Office, Audit Office. Accounts 1/2339 to 2392. (Great Wardrobe 1558–1630) & 3/1106 to 1121 (various, 1559–1662).

Published Sources

(Publication is in London except where otherwise stated.)

BARCLAY, ALEXANDER. (1) The Ship of Fools. (1508/9.) Edn. 1874. (2) The Eclogues [c. 1513]. E.E.T.S. Orig. Series No. 175.(1928.)

BECK, S. WILLIAM. *The Drapers' Dictionary*. Warehousemen and Drapers Journal office, n.d.

BLOUNT, THOMAS ('T.B.'). *Glossographia*. 1656.

BONHAM, SIR WALTER, *see* Kidston.

BOORDE, ANDREW. *A Dyetary of Helth* (1542). Ed. by F. J. Furnivall in E.E.T.S. Extra Series, No. X (1870).

Breton, Nicholas. *A Bower of Delights* . . . (1591). *Works of Nicholas Breton*, ed. A. B. Grosart. 1893.

Chettle, Henry. *Henrie Chettle. Kind-harts dreame* (1592) . . . Bodley Head Quartos, Vol. 4, 1928.

Clifford, Lady Anne, *The Diary of*, ed. V. Sackville-West, 1923.

Cotgrave, Randle. *Dictionaries of the French and English Tongues.* 1611. With additions by R. Sherwood and by J. Howell, 1660.

Debate between Pride and Lowliness (*c.* 1568). Attributed to Francis Thynne; ed. J. P. Collier, *Shakespeare Soc.*, 1841.

Dekker, Thomas. *The Seven Deadly Sins of London.* (1606.) Ed. by H. Brett-Smith, Oxford, 1922.

Donne, John. *Satires* (1594–1600) in *Poems of John Donne* ed. Sir Herbert Grierson 1951.

Drayton, Michael. *Eglogs* (1593) in *Poems of Michael Drayton* ed. J. Buxton, 1953.

Egerton Papers (temp. Q. Elizabeth and James I) ed. J. P. Collier. Camden Soc., 1840.

Elizabeth, Queen. (1) *Court Revels*, see Feuillerat. (2) *Inventory of Wardrobe* (1600). See Nichols, *Progresses etc.* Vol. 3, p. 500. (1823.) (3) *New Year Gifts* (1562–1600). Ibid. Vols. 1 and 2.

Elizabeth of York. Privy Purse Expenses (1523) . . . ed. Sir N. H. Nicolas, 1830.

Elyot, Sir Thomas. *Bibliotheca Eliotae.* (A Latin-English Dictionary 1542. Ed. by T. Cooper, 2nd. edn. 1552 fol.)

England in the Reign of Henry VIII. E.E.T.S. Extra Series, 32. (1878.) Pt. I. Starkey's Life and Letters, ed. S. J. Herrtage; Pt. II Dialogue between Cardinal Pole and Thomas Lupset by Thomas Starkey, ed. J. M. Cowper.

Feuillerat, Albert, (ed). (1) *Documents relating to the office of the Revels in the time of Q. Elizabeth.* 1908. (2) *Ditto in the time of Edward VI and Queen Mary.—The Loseley MSS.* 1914.

Foxe, John. '*Book of Martyrs*' Vol. II (with woodcuts). Edns. 1563 and 1576.

Fuller, Thomas. *The Worthies of England* (1662). Ed. John Freeman, 1952.

Fulwell, Ulpian. . . . . . *Like will to like,* . . . (1568). In *Dodsley's Old plays*, ed. Hazlitt, Vol. 3. (1874.)

GAGE. Household Goods of Sir John Gage. *Sussex Archaeological Collections*. Vol. 45. (Sussex Archaeological Society.)

Gammer Gurton's Needle (1552–1563). ? by Wm. Stevenson. *In Dodsley's Old Plays*, ed. Hazlitt, Vol. 3. (1874.)

GASGOIGNE, GEORGE (1525?–1577). *Complete Works*, ed. J. W. Cunliffe, 1904.

GOOSECAP. *Sir Gyles Goosecappe, Knight. A comedie* . . . (1606) ed. A. H. Bullen in *A Collection of Old English Plays*, vol. 3. (1882.)

GOSSEN, STEPHEN. *Pleasant Quippes for Upstart New-fangled Gentlewomen* . . . (1595). Reprinted, 1847.

Great Orphan Book, The. Notes and Abstracts of, by T. P. Wadley (Wills 1379–1674, in Council House, Bristol.) Bristol and Glos. Archaeol. Soc. 1882–6.

GREENE, ROBERT. *The Black Bookes Messenger* (1592) and *'Cuthbert Conny-Catcher'* . . . (1592) in Bodley Head Quartos No. 10, 1924. *The Honourable Historie of Friar Bacon and Friar Bungay* (1594) ed. G. B. Harrison, 1927.

GRIMSTON, EDWARD. *Narrative of his captivity in the Bastille and his escape* (in 1559) ed. Henry Reeve. London, Philobiblon Soc. *Bibliog. and Hist. Misc.* Vol. 13. (1854.)

HALL, JOSEPH. *Bishop Hall's Satires* (1598).

HALLE, EDWARD. *Hall's Chronicle* (1548). Edn. 1809.

HALLIWELL (HALLIWELL-PHILLIPPS) J. O. *Dictionary of Archaic and Provincial Words*. 6th Edn. 1904.

HARMAN, THOMAS. *A Caveat or Warening for Commen Cursetors*. (3rd edn. 1567) in *Rogues and Vagabonds* . . . ed. E. Viles and F. J. Furnivall (Gollancz, 1907; E.E.T.S. 1880).

HARRISON, WILLIAM. *Harrison's Description of England . . . from Holinshed's Chronicle* . . . *1577, 1587* by F. J. Furnivall, 1877.

HENRY VIII. (1) *Privy Purse Expenses* 1529–32. See Nicolas. (2) *'Wardrobe Account'* (The King's Warrants in 1535/6). Extracts by John Caley, *Archaeologia* Vol. 9, pp. 244–252. See also unpublished MSS.

HEYRICKE LETTERS. *Trans. of Leicestershire Architect. and Archaelog. Soc.* (now *Archaeol. and Hist: Soc.*) Vol. 2. (1866).

HEYWOOD, JOHN. *The Four PP* (c. 1533) ed. J. S. Farmer, 1905.

HOWARD. *Selections from the Household Books of Ld. W. Howard of Naworth Castle.* Newcastle, Surtees Soc. *Pubns.* Vol. 68 (1878).

HUNGERFORD. Inventory of Dame Agnes Hungerford (1523). *Archaeologia*, vol. 38 pt. 2.

JONSON, BEN. Plays, especially *Everyman Out of His Humour* (1599).

JUNIUS, ADRIANUS AND HIGINS, J. *The Nomenclator* edn. 1585.

KIDSTON, G. J. *The Bonhams of Wiltshire and Essex.* Devizes. 1948.

LELAND, JOHN. *J. Lelandi . . . Collectanea . . .* ed. T. Hearne. Edn. 1770.

LENNARD, SIR THOMAS. *An Account of the Families of Lennard and Barrett*, 1908.

LESTRANGE . . . *Accounts of the Lestranges of Hunstanton* (1519–1578). ed. David Gurney in *Archaeologia* Vol. 25, 411–569.

LINDSAY (Lyndesay), SIR DAVID. *Ane Supplicatioun anent syde taillis* (1539–1541). *Ane Dialogue . . . (The Monarche) c.* 1559. Both in *Works of . . . Lindsay*, ed. D. Hamer, Vol. 1., (1931.)

London Prodigal (anonymous comedy, temp. Shakespeare) in *The Ancient British Drama*, 1810.

LYLY (OR LILLY), JOHN. *Endimion the Man in the Moone* (1591); *Midas* (1592); (comedies). *Complete Works of John Lyly.* Oxford, 1902.

MACHYN. *Diary of Henry Machyn, . . . Merchant Taylor . . . from 1550 to 1563.* Camden Soc. No. 48 (1848).

MARSTON, JOHN. *The Scourge of Villainie . . . Satyres.* 1590.

MARTYR. Expenses of Peter Martyr and Bernardinus Ochin (in 1547). *Archaeologia* Vol. 21, p. 489.

MARY, QUEEN. Revels at Court in time of, see Feuillerat.

MIDDLETON MSS. *See* Willoughby Accounts.

MORE, SIR THOMAS. *The Supplycacyon of Soulys* (1529).

MORYSON, FYNES. *An Itinerary* (1605–1617). Edn. Glasgow, MacLehose, 1907.

NARES, ROBERT. *A Glossary* (particularly for literature of Shakespearian times). Ed. J. Halliwell and T. Wright, 1905.

NASH(E), THOMAS. *Pierce Penilesse his Supplication . . .* (1592) in G. Hibbard's *Three Elizabethan pamphlets*, 1951. *Christ's Tears over Jerusalem* (1593). *Have with you to Saffron-Walden* (1596).

NICHOLS, JOHN. *Illustrations of the Manners and Expences . . . 15th, 16th and 17th centuries*, 1797.

> *Progresses, Public Processions etc. of Queen Elizabeth.* Edn. 1823.

NICOLAS, SIR NICHOLAS. *Testamenta Vetusta: . . . Wills . . . from the Reign of Henry II to the Accession of Q. Elizabeth.* 1826. *Privy Purse Expenses.* See Elizabeth of York and Henry VIII.

NORTH. Extracts from the Household Books of Lord North (1575/6). *Archaeologia*, Vol. 19, pp. 283–301.

PALSGRAVE, JOHN. *Lesclarissement de la langue Francoyse* (1530). Pubd. by F. Génin, Paris, 1852.

PLATERUS, THOMAS (the younger). *Thomas Platter's Travels in England in 1599.* Trans. C. Williams. 1937.

PRECEDENCE. *A Copie* [made c. 1587] *of a Boke of Precedence, in* E.E.T.S. Extra Series No. 8 (1869). Ceremonial and Mourning Attire.

RICH(E), BARNABY. *Barnaby Rich's Farewell to Militarie profession . . .* (1581). Shakespeare Society, 1846.

ROWLANDS, SAMUEL. *Look to it, for Ile Stabbe ye* (1604).

> *Martin Mark-all.* (1610.) Various satirical works.

RUTLAND, MSS. of the Duke of. Household Accounts in Vol. 4. Hist. MSS. Commission (1905.)

Shropshire Archaeol. and Nat. Hist. Soc. Trans. Vol. 2. Shrewsbury, 1879. (pp. 400–403 A tradesman's invoice to Sir Wm. Maurice, 1594.)

STARKEY, THOMAS. See *England in the Reign of Henry VIII.*

STOW, JOHN. *The Annales of England . . .* Edns. 1592, 1600.

STUBBES, PHILIP. *The Anatomie of Abuses in England* (1583, 1595) ed. F. J. Furnivall, 1877–8.

Sumptuary Laws. See *Egerton Papers* for the decree of 1579 and notes on others.

THYNNE, FRANCIS. *Animadversions . . .* (1599) ed. G. H. Kingsley. E.E.T.S. Orig. Series No. 9 reissued 1898. See also *Debate between Pride and Lowliness.*

Woolhope Naturalists' Field Club Transactions. Hereford.

Willoughby Household Accounts [16th century] in *Report on the MSS. of Lord Middleton . . .* Hist. MSS. Commission No. 69 (1911).

Wills and Inventories . . . of the northern counties. Surtees Soc. Pubns.
  Vols. 2 and 38. Newcastle, 1835, 1929.
Wills:
  Durham Wills (ibid.).
  Essex Wills at Canterbury. (*Essex Archaeol. Soc. Trans.* vol. 21.)
    Colchester.
  Lancashire and Cheshire Wills and Inventories. *Chetham Soc.
    Pubns.* Nos. 33, 51, 54. Manchester, 1857–61.
  Leeds. R. B. Cook. *Wills of Leeds and District* in *Thoresby Soc.
    Pubns.* vol. 22 (1915).
  Lincoln Wills. (*Pubns. of the Lincoln Record Soc.*) Lincoln.
  London. Calendar of Wills proved in the Court of Hustings A.D.
    1258–1688, ed. R. S. Sharpe, 1889.
  Walthamstow. George S. Fry's *Abstracts of Wills relating to
    Walthamstow, Essex, 1335–1559.* Walth. Antiquarian Soc.
    pubn. No. 9 (1921).
  Wayman, James H. Bloom's *Wayman Wills . . . preserved in . . .
    Canterbury, 1383–1821.* (1922.)

B. SECONDARY

ANTHONY, PEGARET AND ARNOLD, JANET. *Costume, a General
  Bibliography*, Victoria and Albert Museum, 1968.
BECK, S. WILLIAM. *Drapers' Dictionary* . . . (Warehousemen
  and Drapers Jour., 1886). *Gloves* . . . Hamilton, Adams, 1883.
BOEHN, MAX VON. *Modes and Manners* (Vol. 3 on 16th c.) Trans.
  J. Joshua, 1934.
BOUCHER, FRANÇOIS. *A History of Costume in the West.* (N.B.
  Plates.) 1967.
CLINCH, GEORGE. *English Costume* . . . *to the End of the 18th c.,*
  1909.
COTMAN, JOHN S. *Engravings of Sepulchral Brasses in Norfolk and
  Suffolk.* 2 vols. fol., 2nd Edn. 1839.
ESDALE, K. A. *English Monumental Sculpture since the Renaissance,*
  1927. *English Church Monuments, 1510–1840,* 1946.
FAIRHOLT, F. W. *Costume in England*, ed. H. A. Dillon, 1909.
  2 vols.

GARDNER, ARTHUR. *Alabaster Tombs of the Pre-Reformation Period in England*, 1940.

HALL, HERBERT. *Society in the Elizabethan Age*.

HIND, ARTHUR. *Engraving in England*. Vol. 1 *The Tudor Period*, 1952.

Holbein. K. T. Parker. *The Drawings of Hans Holbein . . . at Windsor Castle*, 1945.

Holbein. *The Paintings of Hans Holbein. First complete edition by Paul Ganz*. (Trans.) Phaidon Press, 1950.

Journal of the Royal Society of Arts.

KELLY, FRANCIS. *Shakespearian Costume for Stage and Screen*, 1938 (2nd edn. by A. Mansfield in press).

KELLY, FRANCIS AND SCHWABE, RANDOLPH. *A Short History of Costume and Armour . . . 1066–1800*. 1931. *Historic Costume 1490–1790* (1925).

LEICESTER Museums and Art Gallery. *Hans Eworth, a Tudor Artist and His Circle*, 1965.

LINTHICUM, M. C. *Costume in the Drama of Shakespeare and his Contemporaries*, 1936.

NEVINSON, J. H. *Catalogue of English Domestic Embroidery*, Victoria and Albert Museum.

Oxford English Dictionary.

PITON, CAMILLE. *Le Costume Civil en France du XIII au XIX Siècle*. Paris. (n.d.).

PLANCHÉ, J. R. *Cyclopaedia of Costume . . .*, 1876.

REDFERN, WILLIAM. *Royal and Historic Gloves and Shoes*, 1904.

STRONG, ROY. *Tudor and Jacobean Portraits*, H.M.S.O., 1969.

STRUTT, JOSEPH. *A complete View of the Dress and Habits of the People of England*. 1796–99. (Some inaccuracy.)

Victoria and Albert Museum. *Catalogue of Rubbings of Brasses. . . .*

WILSON, JOHN DOVER, *Life in Shakespeare's England*. Edn. 1949.

Note *also* the relevant volumes in the following:
1. *Costume in the Western World*, ed. J. Laver.
2. *The Folger Shakespeare Library Booklets*.
3. *The Oxford History of English Art*, ed. T. S. R. Boase.
4. *The Pelican History of Art*, ed. N. B. L. Pevsner.

Sources of the Illustrations

Frontispiece. Painting by J. Hoefnagel at Hatfield House. Detail. (Reproduced by kind permission of the Marquess of Salisbury.)

1. Holbein. Benedikt von Hertenstein. *Metropolitan Museum, New York.*
2. Portrait of a Young Man. Artist unknown. *Hampton Court.*
3. Prince Edward (afterwards Edward VI). Artist unknown. *Windsor Castle.*
4. School of Holbein. Henry VIII. *Duke of Devonshire. Chatsworth.*
5. Brass. *Paston church, Norfolk.* (Cotman).
6. (a) Brass. *Ogbourne St. George, Wilts.* (Kites' 'Monumental Brasses of Wiltshire').

   (b) Brass. *Necton church, Norfolk.* (Cotman).
7. (a) B.M. MS. Roy. 16 F II, f. 188. Poems of Charles of Orleans.

   (b) Carving on pillar in *Boxgrove Chantry, Sussex.*
8. (a) From a contemporary drawing in the archives of the Abbey of St. John Baptist, Colchester, Dec. 1. A.D. 1539. Probably copied from Lucas van Leyden's 'Triumph of Mordecai' dated 1515. (drawn by T. W. Warne).

   (b) Horse attendant from Tournament Roll, College of Arms. Reproduced in Henry Shaw's 'Dresses and Decorations of the Middle Ages' Vol. 2.
9. Guillim Stretes. Henry Howard, Earl of Surrey. *Hon. Clive Pearson,* Parham Paik.
10. (a) Terracotta bust of Henry VII. *Victoria and Albert Museum.*

    (b) Terracotta bust of Sir Gilbert Talbot. *Victoria and Albert Museum.*

    (c) Weeper on tomb of Sir Richard Vernon. *Tong Church.*
11. (a) Holbein. Sir Thomas Elyot. *Windsor Castle.*

    (b) Holbein. Sir Henry Guildford. *Detroit Institute of Arts.*
12. Portrait of Prince Arthur, from engraving in Clinch's 'English Costume' after an anon. painting, *Windsor Castle.*
13. (a) Holbein. Sir Nicholas Carew. *Duke of Buccleuch.*

    (b) Holbein. Sir Nicholas Poyntz. *Earl of Harrowby.*
14. Holbein. Gentleman unknown. *Windsor Castle.*
15. (a) Holbein. John More the younger. *Windsor Castle.*

    (b) Holbein. John Russell, Earl of Bedford. *Windsor Castle.*
16. (a) and (b) Holbein. Details from altarpiece, with family of Jacob Meyer, *Darmstedt.*

    (c) From Shaw, H. After a painting by Holbein in *the Louvre.*

17. (a) Brass at *Worlingham church, Suffolk.* (Cotman).
    (b) Brass at *Rougham church, Norfolk.* (Cotman).
18. (a) Brass at *Necton church, Norfolk.* (Cotman).
    (b) Brass at *Maddermarket church, Norwich.* (Cotman).
19. Holbein. Cecily Heron. *Windsor Castle.*
20. (a) Brass at *St. Andrew's church, Norwich.* (Cotman).
    (b) Brass at *Hawkeddon church, Suffolk.* (Cotman).
21. Holbein. English Noblewoman. *British Museum.*
22. Holbein. Jane Seymour. *Vienna. Kunsthistorisches Museum.*
23. Holbein. Queen Catherine Howard. *Museum of Art, Toledo, Ohio, U.S.A.*
24. B.M. MS. Harl. 6064, f. 92.
25. Brass at *Denston church, Suffolk.* (Cotman).
26. (a) From Kelly and Schwabe 'Historic Costume'.
    (b) Brass at *Frense church, Norfolk.* (Cotman).
    (c) Portrait of a Lady. *Ickworth.* (See E. Farrer, 'Portraits in Suffolk Houses').
27. After a portrait of Barbara Yelverton. *Connoisseur,* Vol. 31. Oct. 1911.
28. Holbein. Lady Mary Guildford. *Fine Art Museum, St. Louis, U.S.A.*
29. (a) Follower of Holbein. A Lady unknown. *T. W. Fitzwilliam.*
    (b) Hans Eworth. Queen Mary. *Society of Antiquaries, London.*
30. (a) Holbein. A Lady unknown. *Windsor Castle.*
    (b) Holbein. A Lady unknown. *Windsor Castle.*
31. (a) Holbein. Wife of a Court official of King Henry VIII. *Kunsthistorisches Museum, Vienna.*
    (b) Holbein miniature. Mrs. Pemberton. *Victoria and Albert Museum.*
32. (a) Holbein. Lady with squirrel, and starling. *Marquess of Cholmondeley.*
    (b) Holbein. Unknown young girl. *County Museum, Los Angeles.*
33. (a) The Master 'A. W.' Margaret Countess of Lennox. *University of London, Courtauld Gallery.*
    (b) 'Joueuse de Guitare'. *Bibliothèque Nationale, Paris.* from 'Le Costume Civil en France'. C. Piton.
34. Federigo Zuccaro. Robert Dudley, Earl of Leicester. Artist unknown. *National Portrait Gallery, London.*
35. Sir Philip Sidney. Artist unknown. *National Portrait Gallery.*
36. (a) and (b) Foxe's 'Book of Martyrs', Edn. 1563, pp. 1209 and 1544.
37. François Clouet. Charles IX. *The Louvre, Paris.*
38. Sir A. Mor. Hugh, 4th son of John Fitz-william of Sprotborough. *Peterborough Museum.*
39. (a) and (b) Foxe's 'Book of Martyrs', Edn. 1563.
    (a) p. 1205 John Bradford, preacher and martyr.
    (b) p. 1353.
    (c) Engraving after T. Lant in *Funeral Procession of Sir Phillip Sidney.*
40. Engraving by Holl of portrait of Thomas Howard, fourth Duke of Norfolk. *Arundel Castle.*

41. All from Foxe's 'Book of Martyrs', Edn. 1563.
    (a) p. 1144.
    (b) p. 1080.
    (c) p. 1037.
42. (a) 'La Ligue' (detail). ? *School of Pourbus. Carnavalet Museum.* From 'Le Costume civil en France'. C. Piton.
    (b) From 'La Première Partie du Compte de Richard Cooke'. *The Folger Shakespeare Library* (see 'Elizabethan Pageantry').
    (c) Sketch of one way of wearing the Mandilion, from Kelly and Schwabe.
43. Sir Philip Sidney (?). Artist unknown. *National Portrait Gallery.*
44. (a) Robert Devereux, second Earl of Essex. Artist unknown. *National Portrait Gallery.*
    (b) John Gerarde, portrait from his 'Herbal'.
45. Cornelis Ketel. Sir Christopher Hatton.
46. M. Gheeraerts. Robert Devereux, second Earl of Essex. *Duke of Bedford*
47. Sir Francis Drake, artist unknown. *Greenwich National Maritime Museum.*
48. James I of England and VI of Scotland. Artist unknown. *National Portrait Gallery.*
49. Cornelis Ketel. Sir Martin Frobisher. *Bodleian Library, Oxford.*
50. (a) Isaac Oliver. A young Man. *Windsor Castle.*
    (b) Adapted from Kelly's 'Shakesperian Costume'.
    (c) From Abraham De Bruyn's 'Habitas Variarum Gentium'.
51. (a) James Stewart, Earl of Murray. Engraving. *Holyrood House, Edinburgh.*
    (b) James Douglas, Earl of Morton. Engraving.
    (c) French school. Antoine de La Marck. *Bibliothèque Nationale, Paris.*
52. (a) Sir John Hawkins, artist unknown. *City Museum and Art Gallery, Plymouth.*
    (b) Engraving. Edward de Vere, 17th Earl of Oxford.
53. (a) Isaac Oliver. The three brothers Browne and their page. *The Marquess of Exeter.*
    (b) Alexander Nowell. Artist unknown. *Bodleian Library, Oxford.*
54. Sir Henry Unton. *E. Peter Jones.*
55. (a) and (b) Brass of John and Susan Selwyn. *Walton-on-Thames church,* photograph (drawn by T. W. Warne).
56. Princess Elizabeth (afterwards Queen Elizabeth I), artist unknown. *Windsor Castle.*
57. Sitter and artist unknown. *National Portrait Gallery.*
58. Federigo Zucchero. ? Mary Stuart. *Duke of Devonshire.*
59. Hans Eworth. Princess Mary Tudor. *Fitzwilliam Museum, Cambridge.*
60. Queen Elizabeth I, artist unknown. *National Portrait Gallery.*
61. Brass. *Beerstreet church, Norfolk.* (Cotman).
62. Queen Elizabeth I. Engraving. (Photograph kindly supplied by Arthur M. Hind. See his book 'Engravings in England in the 16th and 17th Centuries. I. Tudor Period.')

63. (a) and (b) Different views of Dame Anne Petre. *Tomb in Ingatestone church, Essex.*
64. (a) Brass. *St. Margaret's church, Norwich.* (Cotman).
    (b) Brass. *St. Thomas's church, Salisbury.* (Kites' 'Monumental Brasses of Wiltshire').
65. P. Oudry (attributed). Mary, Queen of Scots. *National Portrait Gallery.*
66. (a) Clouet. Elizabeth of Austria. *The Louvre, Paris.*
    (b) French school. Princesse de Condé. *Bibliothèque Nationale, Paris.*
67. John Gower. Elizabeth Lady Kytson. *Tate Gallery.*
68. (a) Brass. *Felbrigg church, Norfolk* (Cotman).
    (b) Katherine, wife of Sir John Spencer. *Tomb in Great Brington church, Northamptonshire.*
69. (a) and (c) Adapted from Kelly's 'Shakespearian Costume'.
    (b) From photograph of late 16th century Gloves.
70. (a) M. Gheeraerts. Mary Countess of Dorset. *Knole.*
    (b) Alonso Sanchez Coello. Portrait of a girl (detail). Reproduced in *Connoisseur*, April, 1938.
    (c) Federigo Zuccaro. Queen Elizabeth I. *Gallery of Fine Arts, Yale University, U.S.A.*
71. (a) From drawing in Fairholt's 'Costume in England', vol. 1.
    (b) B.M. MS. Add. 28330.
    (c) French school. Demoiselles Françaises. *Department of Engravings, the Louvre, Paris.*
72. (a) George Turberbile. 'Booke of Falconrie'.
    (b) Woodcut in 'The Orchard and the Garden'. London, Islip, 1594.
    (c) Foxe's 'Book of Martyrs', Edn. 1563, p. 277.
    (d) Ibid., p. 249.
73 and 74. Cesare Vecellio. 'Habite Antichi e Moderni', Edn. Venice. 1598.
75. Foxe's 'Book of Martyrs', Edn. 1563.
    (a) and (c) p. 1387.
    (b) and (d) p. 1706.
    (e) p. 474.
76. Marc Gheeraerts the elder. Countess of Leicester and her children (detail). *Lord de L'Isle and Dudley, Penshurst.*

Index

Numbers in Italics indicate *page* references to illustrations.
Materials used in 16th c. costumes are listed in the glossary, pp. 212–227. Those used for any particular garment are generally to be found at the end of its description.
Colours used are listed on pp. 214–216;
Furs on pp. 218–220.